DENIS LAW'S SOCCER SPECIAL

DENIS LAW'S

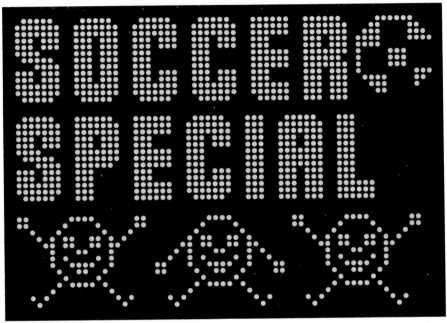

Illustrations by Joe Wright and Kevin Hudson

Willow Books
Collins
Grafton Street, London
1983

Willow Books
William Collins & Co Ltd
London Glasgow Sydney Auckland
Toronto Johannesburg

Law, Denis
Denis Law's soccer special
1. Soccer – Great Britain
I. Title
796.334'0941   GV944.G7

ISBN 0 00 218004 9

First published 1983
Copyright © Denis Law and Ron Gubba 1983

Made by Lennard Books
Mackerye End
Harpenden, Herts AL5 5DR

Editor Michael Leitch
Designed by David Pocknell's Company Ltd
Production Reynolds Clark Associates Ltd
Printed and bound in Spain by
TONSA, San Sebastian

CONTENTS

INTRODUCTION

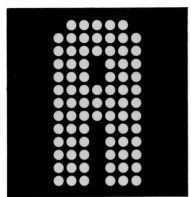

ha!' said Mr Eddie Brennan, assistant secretary of Huddersfield Town FC, 'so this is the lad.' He placed an encouraging hand on the shoulder of my brother George.

'No, no!' cried George.

'No, no!' added John, another of my brothers, who had also made the long trek south that day from Aberdeen, for purposes of fraternal protection, moral support and looking after the railway tickets.

'It's him,' explained George and John together.

'Oh!' said Mr Brennan, turning to look at the third Law brother, a skinny bespectacled fifteen-year-old article, name of Denis.

My brothers and I now waited while the assistant secretary of this historic, if slightly fallen, football club – founded 1908, FA Cup winners 1922, Division I champions 1923–24, 1924–25, 1925–26, since when not a lot – focused on the most recent trialist to present himself at the Leeds Road ground. Being a polite man, he kept silent while the input section of his brain recorded a stunted blond creature barely five feet tall, weighing about eight stone, owl-like glasses clamped to his nose, a pronounced squint in his right eye . . .

To the object of his gaze – me – it felt more like the end than the beginning. Then the assistant secretary nodded in an understanding way, and I switched to thinking that maybe things were not so bad. After all, given a start like that, life could only get better. And it did get better. Several minutes later we all met the manager of the club, Andy Beattie – and he hardly looked at me at all! Was this acceptance? Not quite, but the rest of the trial went well enough, and a fortnight later I signed official forms and became a groundstaff apprentice. I was, in a manner of speaking, launched.

That was in 1955. Since then, I have knocked around in the game from Maine Road, Manchester to Turin and back to Old Trafford, worn the Scottish jersey with pride and some honour, done battle with South American footballers and, more recently, with radio and television equipment. Some fragments of these experiences will remain with me for ever, like bits of old shrapnel. Traces of them have surfaced in this book, together with a heap of other thoughts, memories and favourite stories about the game and the galaxy of characters it has produced over the years – and keeps on producing with each new season. Nearly all the stories are true, so far as I know. We've changed one or two of the names, but I doubt if this will make much difference. Inside soccer, secrets never last very long.

BRUSHES, BROOMS AND LEATHER CASEYS

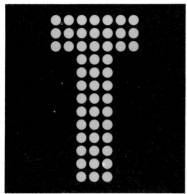

hey had people like groundstaff apprentices back in Victorian times. You may have seen them in late-night horror movies, or on children's television, hiding in terror from the evil villain while he lurches about in some rotten attic. Ragged urchins they were, surrounded by dense smoke and fog, and they gathered their pennies as mudlarks and crossing sweepers, or slaved for costermongers, street entertainers and coal heavers; they slept where they dropped and were always hungry.

The main difference between those Victorian apprentices and the groundstaff boys of the 1950s was that, while the 19th-century crowd tended to specialize, we did everything. Boots, terraces, toilets, offices – if the guvnor wanted it scrubbed, polished or painted, we did it. Fortunately for the clubs, there was never any shortage of starry-eyed applicants – or starry-eyed parents hovering in the background. So the clubs never had to advertise, and the true nature of an apprentice's work never quite dawned on the chosen few until they found themselves on a wet Monday morning, maybe hundreds of miles from home, with a broom in one hand facing a gigantic terrace, every step of which was paved with cigarette packets, crisp packets, sweet wrappers, dogends and larger rainsodden lumps that were better left unidentified.

Monday morning on the terraces – that was where the apprentices' week began. We gathered the match-day litter into mounds, then squashed it into sacks and burned it in a large incinerator at the back of the stadium. In addition to the litter we swept from the terraces, there was always plenty of rubbish to be collected from the club offices. One day I was piling handfuls of it onto the fire when I noticed some familiar-looking pieces of green paper curling up in the flames. They were pound notes! Somehow they had got mixed up with the rubbish and I was burning them.

I have no idea how many had already gone up in smoke, but a quick check of the sack I was emptying at the time revealed several large brown envelopes, all stuffed with cash. They had come down from the secretary's office, but just how they came to be mixed up with the rubbish remains a mystery. I do know that we rescued a lot of money that day, far more than I had ever set eyes on before, but the fact that I was working with the head groundsman at the time meant that the honesty of a poor trawlerman's son was not put to the test. I've often wondered!

As a kid, I had not owned a pair of proper football boots until the Christmas before my arrival in Huddersfield; my family had not been able to afford any. Now I had dozens of pairs to look after, because cleaning the boots of every member of every team was just part of the apprentice's job. As a chore it was distinctly better than another of our duties – cleaning out the public toilets.

I will not linger over every item we discovered in those evil-smelling bunkers. Instead, you may be more interested in something that happened a few seasons ago at the ground of Plymouth Argyle. They had been drawn at home to Everton in the third round of the FA Cup and, not surprisingly, the game attracted a record attendance. Also present were a squad of pickpockets who went to work on the crowd during the match. On the Monday morning, the groundstaff discovered 106 empty wallets stuffed in the plumbing.

Anyone for water polo?

The highlight of those early days was the one day a week when we played football for the junior team at nearby Heckmondwike. Even this outing had its problems. One was the canal which ran along one side of the pitch. Every so often the ball would end up in its murky waters, and, as it was a highly precious object – in fact the only football we possessed – whoever kicked it in had to go and retrieve it. There was a long pole which we preferred to use for this purpose, but if the pole would not reach the ball then the kicker had to slide himself into the freezing water and collect the ball personally. As I could not swim the prospect of having to go into the canal terrified me; fortunately, on the few occasions it was down to me, my mate Gordon Low, who knew of my problem, gallantly stood in for me.

Then there was the ball itself. Football equipment has changed a great deal in recent years, and the balls used today are very different from the leather-panelled 'casey' that we had to use. Those old leather balls had a massive capacity for soaking up moisture. If you were playing on a wet pitch, which most of the time we were, the ball soon became heavy and difficult to kick any distance. Delicate chips and lobs were seen less often in those days. In fact, if you could take a corner-kick and reach the edge of the penalty area, you were in the team. I sometimes hear it said that the players of yesterday would find it hard to survive in today's game, but when you think of the skills displayed by the likes of Finney and Matthews with the old leather ball, you can only be amazed that they managed to do half the things they did.

Possibly the biggest problem of all with the leather ball was heading it. You had to be a very brave lad indeed to jump for the casey when it was soaking wet and weighing a ton. There was also the problem of the lacing, which kept the leather case fastened tight

over the rubber inner tube. Anyone bold enough, or dumb enough, to head the ball risked ramming his forehead into the lace which could well remove several inches of skin, and frequently did. Being a devout coward, I never headed the ball in training. I saved all my resolve and determination for the job of heading it during a match.

Like the dodo, groundstaff apprentices are now extinct. Gone are the days when a promising schoolboy would kick a ball against the outside wall of a football club and dream 'If only I could get in there.' The shortage of class players and the search for ever younger and younger talent means that today club scouts are 'tapping up' young players long before they leave school. There is no longer that feeling of awe about a football club in a young boy's mind. Nor does he need to serve an apprenticeship sweeping the terraces and cleaning the toilets – someone else can do that. Today, youngsters in sharp suits turn up on match days to be wined and dined while parents and management negotiate. The question now is not 'How do I get in?' but 'How much can dad screw out of the club?'

CLUBLAND

football club is rather like a large family. There are those that are well-to-do, and the majority who have a struggle to make ends meet. Just like a family, every club has its own cast of characters, some of them a little larger than life.

Football club directors come in all shapes and sizes. Burnley now have a Bob Lord stand to commemorate the late local butcher who once ruled the club like a tyrant and perhaps represents an almost extinct breed. At the other end of the spectrum, Watford are currently enjoying undreamed-of success under the entrepreneurial talents of pop-singer Elton John. Between these extremes is a wide variety of personalities and styles.

One chairman I knew drove a Rolls Royce, smoked fat cigars and drank champagne by the bucketful. He was the proprietor of a chain of pork-butchers, which was useful when it came to ordering the sausage rolls for the directors' guest room on Saturday afternoons. A feature of team trips abroad was that as the aircraft roared off the end of the runway – almost before it had levelled out – the steward would be rushing along the aisle with the chairman's champagne. The same man had an unusual passion for bananas. Give him a bunch of bananas and a bottle of bubbly and he was your friend for life.

One thing which many directors have in common is that they are successful businessmen outside soccer. It always surprises me, therefore, how few of them bring their business sense to the club boardroom. Men who normally wheel and deal with enormous shrewdness and caution seem to think they are playing with Monopoly money once they lay their hands on the club chequebook. Players are bought for colossal sums and often sold at a massive loss just a few months later. If they ran their regular business the way they run their football club, most of these directors would be bankrupt within a month.

As for having what you might call 'real contact' with the game, I remember one old boy who was on the board at Old Trafford. United were playing an FA Cup-tie away at Barnsley. Midway through the first half we were leading 2–0 but the old boy thought we were two down until someone explained to him that Barnsley were the team playing in red. United, as the away side, had switched to their change strip. The chances of the old director actually recognizing any of his own players were evidently nil.

The club secretary is normally a much sharper individual. He (or sometimes she) acts as a sort of substitute mother to many of the players, most of whom have gone straight into football after leaving school. Few have any experience of organizing their own lives and so the secretary acts as a sort of wet nurse. On one famous occasion a key individual arrived at the airport at the start of an important foreign trip without his passport. It needed a desperate dash by taxi to rush the little blue book to the airport; it arrived about a minute before take-off. Now it is standard practice for the club secretary to collect all passports several days before departure – and hang on to them.

Unlike some of his director colleagues, the secretary is generally prudent and constantly on the lookout for ways to earn the club money, or save it. He is happy to carry members of the press if the club flies abroad. There are obvious practical and financial advantages in the arrangement. Occasionally, it even happens that a few supporters are allowed on board as well, particularly where travel behind the Iron Curtain is involved and restrictions are tight.

A few seasons ago, one club was planning a trip to Italy for a European match. Even after the press had been accommodated, there was still a large number of empty seats left on the flight. The secretary saw a golden opportunity to save the club a few pounds by filling up the empty seats with supporters. The trip was a disaster.

The first thing to go wrong was the club's accommodation in Italy, which turned out to be well below par. Then the team lost the match by a disputed goal, late in the game. The trip home was gloomy enough, but the last straw came when some of the travelling fans got drunk and began abusing club officials and players. Within a few weeks, the club had a new secretary.

Nothing says more about a club than the way it travels. Arsenal, for instance, have always been in the caviar-and-champagne league. Today, most of the big clubs have luxury coaches with video and stereo on board and no shortage of good food and drink for the team. If an overnight stop is involved, then it will be at one of the better hotels in the area. Liverpool and Manchester United even have overnight stops before home matches. It's all part of the process of making sure that the players are both mentally and physically in the mood for big matches.

Things are a little different at the opposite end of the social scale. Some of the smaller clubs are still travelling in old 'bangers' and the menu is more likely to consist of a packet of sandwiches and a pork pie, with a can of lager to wash it all down. Overnight stops are avoided like the plague, except on very special occasions such as FA Cup-ties. Teams frequently set off at six or seven in the morning, in order to arrive at a ground at the opposite end of the country just in time for the kick-off. After the match, it's straight back onto the bus, arriving home at maybe four o'clock on a Sunday morning.

Once when I was with United we went through the experience of getting to the ground just a few minutes before kick-off, but it certainly wasn't planned. We were playing Spurs at White Hart Lane, in the first leg of a European Cup-Winners' Cup match. There was so much traffic heading for the ground that our coach was completely blocked. We had to ask for a police escort to get us there in time. We just made it – but only after changing on the coach and running straight out on the pitch when we got there.

We had a different type of police escort, and a different reason for being delayed, when we visited East Berlin to meet Vorwaerts in a European match. Our coach arrived at Checkpoint Charlie in good time and then was kept waiting for hours while the East German security police satisfied themselves that our credentials were in order. We were carrying a number of journalists on the coach and we had a suspicion at the time that it was their passports which were being more closely scrutinized than ours. However, I learned later that when we had all filled in those little identification cards everyone gets when entering a foreign country, my good friend Paddy Crerand had added an extra card. Under the heading 'Name', he had written 'James Bond'. Under 'Reason for Visit' he had put 'Espionage'. And somebody out there must have believed him!

The Boss

Perhaps the most important person in any club is the manager. He is almost always a former player and he eats, sleeps and drinks football. When his own team isn't playing he can usually be found in another club's director's box sizing up future opponents, or running the rule over a player he might want to buy. With so many mid-week matches nowadays, the mugs of Bovril and hot pies in the guest room are more likely to be consumed by visiting managers than by any other form of guest.

Managerial styles differ widely, from the flamboyance of Brian Clough and Malcolm Allison to the quietly methodical ways of Bob Paisley. What matters most is the manager's motivating ability. Even the best players cannot perform to their best standard if their motivation is wrong.

Bill Shankly may well have been the greatest motivator of all time. He had a way of getting teams to feel that they were better than the opposition, whoever that opposition happened to be. There was a story that in the Sixties he used Subbuteo men on a board to represent the opposing team. He would then go through the team, man for man, highlighting what he saw as their weaknesses.

Once, Chelsea were the visitors to Anfield. At the time, the Pensioners were riding high in the First Division and it looked like being a hard match. Bill is said to have begun his pre-match team talk with the words: 'This Chelsea, they're a great team . . . look at them.' He indicated the Subbuteo men on the board. 'Let's just have a look at them individually.' Beginning with the goalkeeper, he then went through the whole eleven, finding some fault with every single one. Then came the dramatic gesture. 'Ach, they're a load of rubbish,' he said, sweeping the plastic men onto the floor. 'We can beat them easily.' The result was that Shanks's team then went on to the field feeling ten feet tall and fearing no-one.

He occasionally carried this belief in his own team to outrageous lengths. Earlier in his career, when he was my manager at Huddersfield, we played a match against Charlton and were annihilated 5–1. In the dressing-room after the match he kept repeating that he couldn't understand how we had come to be beaten. 'They were rubbish,' he kept saying. Shanks could only ever see one team on the field – his own.

Medicine man

Trainers, or coaches as they now tend to be called, are often among the most popular characters at any club. No one symbolizes the tradition of the wet Saturday afternoon more than the man running onto the pitch with his bag of secrets to attend the wounded.

It is not a widely kept secret that such bags generally contain two essential items of medieval torture – the magic sponge and the smelling salts. In its day, the magic sponge has been used to cure just about everything from an ingrowing toenail to a broken leg. Its apparently miraculous healing powers are easy to explain. Ice cold water applied to almost any part of the bare anatomy on a freezing day is calculated to bring an ailing patient very quickly back from the dead. If it fails, the smelling salts are brought into play. These either lift the top of a man's head off, or at the very least take his mind instantly off all other pain.

The trainer is also responsible for seeing that the players train. Unfortunately, some of us at Old Trafford couldn't see eye to eye about the way this should be done.

Our trainer was United's former goalkeeper Jack Crompton – Crompo to the lads. He liked to do things by the book, which meant getting through a whole lot of running and sprinting before we were able to play with the ball. Paddy Crerand and I hated all that. We weren't at all keen on fitness training, we just wanted to play with the ball.

Crompo had a habit of turning up at training sessions carrying a couple of bags with a ball tucked under each arm – it made him look a bit like a jug. If Paddy or I got the chance we would sneak up behind him and knock one of the balls free. Then we would run off like a couple of kids and play with it. Sometimes it was a bit like school, with Crompo the angry gym teacher demanding that we bring his ball back. If things went a bit too far, Paddy and I were liable to finish up explaining our conduct to the 'headmaster' – Matt Busby.

Not being allowed to play with a ball was just one of the odd paradoxes of life at a football club. Another was not being allowed on the pitch between matches. This was the groundsman's patch and he guarded it like a lion. I've seen more 'Keep Off The Grass' signs inside football grounds than in any park.

The treatment room

This is one place where every player ends up sooner or later. When I first came into football, physiotherapy was a straight choice between sitting under a heat lamp or plunging an injured limb alternately into buckets of hot and cold water. Some of the smaller clubs haven't progressed much from that state even today, but most of the large clubs have a battery of machines to cover all eventualities. Machines have in some cases overtaken human skill: when we had a series of power cuts, a few years ago, there were a number of physios who weren't quite sure what to do without their machines.

My first experience of the treatment room came at Huddersfield. In those days, the trainer and the physio were one and the same person. Ours was the former England captain Roy Goodall. The system was that players needing treatment came back to the club in the afternoon, training having been taken by Roy in the morning. Naturally, senior players were seen to first and, being very much a junior at the time, I was the last in the queue.

Eventually my turn came and Roy got my leg under the heat lamp. By now, all the senior players had been seen to and left. I was the last one in the room. After a while Roy went off to attend to some other business, leaving me slowly cooking under the machine. Time began to slip by and my leg began getting hotter but there was no sign of Roy. Eventually I couldn't stand the heat any longer so I took myself off the machine and went to look for the missing physio.

I was amazed to find that I was entirely alone. Roy had apparently forgotten about me and gone home. So had everyone else at the club. The whole place was locked up, with me a prisoner inside. I switched off the heat machine and let myself out through a turnstile.

Ronnie Briggs, our Northern Ireland goalkeeper at Old Trafford, did not take the treatment room over-seriously. One day he went in to have his ankle strapped up. The physio took ages making a neat job of the strapping. Finally, looking pleased with himself, he leant back and said: 'There, how's that?' 'That's terrific,' said Briggs. 'The only trouble is, it's the wrong ankle.'

Some weeks later I saw Briggsy coming out of the treatment room looking bright red, the skin beginning to peel off his face. We had two lamps, one an infra-red, the other ultra-violet, and Briggsy had sat hoping to get a sun tan, under the wrong one.

The scout least likely . . .

The legendary figure of schoolboy dreams is the scout. Those furtive individuals who lurk in the shadows at junior matches, endlessly searching for talent. They do exist, of course, but they go about their business in a more orthodox way than many imagine.

The most unlikely scout I ever met was my father. When I first played as a professional, the maximum wage was still about £14 and the only legal way that the club could pay us any more money was to attach my dad to the coaching staff. This meant he had to send in reports detailing the strengths and weaknesses of junior players he had seen. The joke was that my father had spent forty years at sea and never been to a football match in his life. He knew far more about mackerel than he did about inside-forwards.

Tickets, please

No-one has more power to influence the image of a club than the commissionaires. They are the first people any visitor meets and, on match days, some would say, the first obstacle to be crossed. Not all of them are difficult, of course, but some would not have been out of place in Hitler's SS. It's amazing what effect a uniform has on some people, and how the commissionaires and their behaviour vary from club to club.

Everton, for instance, seem to have more commissionaires than players, and most of them are difficult. A couple of seasons ago I arrived at Goodison Park one afternoon before an evening match. I was there early to do a television interview out on the pitch and I knew that the television crew were inside waiting for me. Because I was early, I had arrived without a ticket which my producer would be bringing later in the day. I was surprised to find a man, who vaguely resembled a military policeman, guarding the door.

'Ticket, please,' he said, as I approached.

I explained that I hadn't got a ticket and why I was there.

'I know who you are,' he said, 'and I know why you are here, but you haven't got a ticket, so you can't come in.'

At first I couldn't believe it, but it soon dawned on me that he

was perfectly serious. In the end I had to go to the ticket office and have a message sent through to the club secretary, who eventually came and explained to the commissionaire that it was all right for me to be admitted.

Rules, of course, are made for a purpose and in general should be obeyed, although the late Douglas Bader also said: 'Rules are for the guidance of wise men and the blind obedience of fools.' Sometimes a little common sense is called for.

When Manchester United opened their players' lounge in the early Sixties, the club was anxious that the place didn't get filled up with people who had no right to be there, and fairly strict rules were applied. Each player was allowed to take in one guest and he was issued with two passes for this purpose: one for himself and one for his guest. One day I had mislaid my own ticket and, when I attempted to go into the room, the commissionaire on the door would not let me pass. It was not a case of mistaken identity, I had simply turned up without my pass and he was not going to let me in. I was flabbergasted. Every Tom, Dick and Harry was inside, most of them complete strangers, but I, the most expensive player in the club's history at the time, couldn't get in. I made it in the end – thanks to an old-fashioned shoulder charge.

Yes, the more I think of it, a football club *is* like a large family. Well, how do *you* get into the bathroom at your place?

FOOTBALL GOES TO THE HAIRDRESSER'S

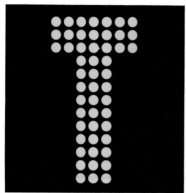

To see how much the game has changed in the last thirty years, you need only to glance at some of the old film footage. Recently I was looking at the 1953 FA Cup final: there was Stanley Matthews, wrapped in baggy black shorts and a shirt two sizes too large which billowed in the wind like the spinnaker on a yacht, mesmerizing the opposition and leading Blackpool to their historic 4–3 win over Bolton.

Everything has changed since then: wages, kit, hairstyles, not to mention the way that the game is played, or the fact that Blackpool, once stalwarts of the First Division, now languish near the bottom of the Fourth. At the time, though, that match was a model of professional football, and to thirteen-year-olds like me the style of play of those Cup finalists was the only one to adopt.

The teams played to a 'W' formation, with orthodox wingers and a spearheading centre-forward, and the numbers on their shirts were complete job descriptions. Full-backs (Nos 2 and 3) marked the wingers (7 and 11); the centre-half (5) looked after the centre-forward (9). Wing-halves (4 and 6) were matched against inside-forwards (8 and 10).

Players wore heavy leather boots, with shinguards the thickness of a Hank Jansen novel wedged in the front of heavy woollen stockings. Hairstyles were of one kind, the regulation short back and sides. The game seemed to be full of characters and, despite the cumbersome kit, numerous outstanding players.

Those were the days of the £10 maximum wage, and none of the team arrived at the ground in a Jaguar or a Mercedes. Outside the Pittodrie Stadium, in my native Aberdeen, you were more likely to see the local heroes arriving on two-wheeled transport; cycle sheds were in greater demand than car parks.

Tank battles

The average player was probably a few pounds heavier than his modern counterpart and his bulky gear made him look a bit like a human tank rumbling around a muddy battlefield. Perhaps because of this, physical collisions seemed to me a good bit more dramatic.

British football has always been noted, of course, for its physical aspect. I've heard it said that in the late Forties, when Manchester United met Arsenal at home and United's own 'Gunner' Jack Rowley clashed with Alex Forbes, the impact could be heard on the other side of town. It was a man's game all right, but somehow the confrontations seemed to lack cynicism.

That tradition was carried on in my own playing days by men like Dave Mackay, who could tackle with enough force to uproot a tree, but always fairly and with a high degree of skill. I remember Dave breaking a leg at Old Trafford in a European Cup Winners' Cup-tie, going for a ball which a lot of players would not have dared to try for. The significant thing, though, was that Dave broke his own leg, not someone else's.

There was, too, my old 'sparring partner', Jack Charlton. 'Big Jack' once announced in a television interview that he kept a little black book in which he recorded the names of players he 'had his eye on'. There were rumoured to be just two names in that infamous little book. I've often wondered whose was the other one.

Jack was certainly a hard man, but in my estimation he was fair. Unfortunately the same could not be said for some of his team-mates in that ambitious Leeds United side, fashioned by Don Revie, who were the pioneers of a new attitude in football which seemed to be based on a policy of 'win at all costs'. They cultivated the so-called art of the 'professional foul' at a time when phrases like 'late tackle' and 'over the ball' were becoming unacceptably common in the language of the game.

The new numbers game

Being a hardened Scot, and as such envious of any success enjoyed by England, I refused to watch their World Cup victory over West Germany in 1966. I have watched it many times since, of course, but I could not bring myself to do so on the day. While the whole English nation was rejoicing on that sunny July afternoon, I was trying to lose myself playing a round of golf, far from radios, television sets or newspapers.

Whether or not I saw the match live is now highly irrelevant. What is important is that England won by embracing a new concept of play which was completely foreign to British crowds and which in a very short space of time would lead to a strangulation of the game I was brought up on. The new style was also responsible for a marked reduction in the number of outstanding players arriving in the game.

Alf Ramsey won the World Cup for England playing a 4–3–3 system and in so doing established a new pattern for clubs to follow. What few people in the game seemed able to realize was that Alf achieved his success because he had a unique collection of individuals at his disposal who could make the system work. Few League clubs were in the same fortunate position.

British football had traditionally sought to use wingers to get down the flanks and behind defences, turning them and creating opportunities for forwards. Alf Ramsey did away with wingers, replacing them with overlapping full-backs. But how many clubs had a pair of full-backs of the calibre of George Cohen and Ray Wilson? England's World Cup final forwards were Alan Ball, Roger Hunt and Geoff Hurst, three men who had both the skill and the inclination to keep moving, making dummy runs and creating gaps. Few clubs had such an inventive trio. Attempts to emulate the England performance would inevitably lead to stagnation in League matches.

To me, the saddest aspect of England's World Cup victory was that there was no place in the team for Jimmy Greaves. It seemed an apt comment on the shape of things to come that in this brave new world of football there was no room for the greatest English player of my generation.

It took a few seasons for the full impact of the changes in the game to be felt; old dogs find it hard to learn new tricks and there were a few of us around who were pretty set in our ways. I can remember when the new method arrived at Old Trafford – yes, even Matt Busby was seduced into giving it a try. Ours, though, was a very loose 4–3–3 formation and, like England, we were in the fortunate position of having one or two above-average players who, despite their instinctive dislike of regimentation, could adapt their game sufficiently to achieve success, whatever the plan. The real damage was being done at grass-roots level where, instead of being encouraged to develop natural skills, youngsters were being drilled into robotic habits.

Soon the numerical systems were all the rage. There was 4–3–3 and 4–4–2 and 4–2–4 and weird variations like 4–3–2–1. It was getting to the point where players needed pocket calculators. I remember one Scottish football writer advocating that the national side should adopt a 4–4–3 formation which, bearing in mind that the goalkeeper normally didn't figure in the arithmetic, meant we should need twelve players on the field. That reporter certainly needed a calculator.

The one undeniable feature of all of these systems was that they placed a greater emphasis on defence than they did on attack. We at Old Trafford had always had a simple philosophy: we didn't mind how many goals our opponents scored, as long as we scored more. If they scored three, we would score four. Now football managements were turning this philosophy on its head. The first priority became to stop the opposition from scoring. Whatever else it was, it was bound to be less entertaining.

Such radical changes in the game led to the creation of that dreaded document, the coaching manual. Then came the coaching courses, and soon an army of new men began to roll off the production line, all armed with pieces of paper called coaching certificates: proof positive that they understood the new system.

These automatons brought with them a new message. Sameness was to be the new creed and method and organization the new virtues. There would be no room in this modern game for the talented individual. Those who did not fit the mould would perish. Soon it would become fashionable to mock rather than praise those few 'eccentrics' who possessed great individual skill: the virtuoso performers who for so long had, in the public mind at least, provided the game's major attraction.

I can remember one manager of this new breed, a man of singularly little real talent, who thought it was smart to state repeatedly that 'stars' were things which shone in the sky and 'flair' was something to have at the bottoms of your trousers. His commitment was, it seemed, to mediocrity; as it happened, it brought the man in question a brief flirtation with the illusion of success, followed quickly by the sack.

Football's new creed also needed a new language and one gradually evolved: appropriately, perhaps, much of the new jargon used words which previously had little or nothing to do with football.

Phrases like 'work rate' and 'doing a job' sounded to me more appropriate to the building trade, while 'getting bodies behind the ball' called up pictures of graveyards. Then there was 'pressure', which players 'piled on', 'soaked up', 'relieved' or 'took off', then 'reapplied'. Now we had a thing called 'a set piece' – was this an import from the furniture trade?

As for the opposition, it was possible to 'contain them' (like sardines in a can?), 'shackle them' (like medieval slaves?) 'close them down' (like the January sales?) or even 'turn them over' (like tired old mattresses?). Players could either 'create space' (like a lumberjack?) or 'find space' (like an astronaut?).

Even the pitch got into the act as we discovered an 'attacking third of the field' and a 'defensive third of the field'; and presumably to give someone the 'freedom of the park' was to allow him to take his dog for a walk. As for the match itself, that could be 'sewn up' – like a mailbag, no doubt.

After the 1983 League Cup final, Bob Paisley was heard to remark that one pundit had spoken to him so much about 'positive' and 'negative' aspects of the game that he began to think he was talking to the Wembley electrician!

Magnet men and substitutes

As the trend towards arithmetical football continued, the arrival of the blackboard at the pre-match team talk was inevitable. When it came to Old Trafford it was not very popular. Matt Busby began using magnetic men on a board to explain the new tactics, and predictably this classroom approach created a classroom-style reaction.

In the middle of the most complex tactical explanation someone would distract the manager's attention while someone else removed one of the pieces from the board. Often, it would take a while for the missing 'man' to be missed. When it was missed, steam would come from Busby's ears. An alternative 'play' was to add an extra man when he was not looking, so that one team then had twelve men, while the other might have only ten. One of the players would then say it was no wonder the tactics worked if one team had more players. Once again, the proverbial cow pat would hit the fan.

A gradual effect of these and other 'mechanizing' processes was to stifle individual talent. This led to a shortage of outstanding players in the game, and as they became harder and harder to find, more and more money was paid for mediocre performers in the hope that somehow these geese might turn out to be swans. Few of them did.

A few seasons ago, they told a story on Merseyside about one such player who had travelled the rounds, changing hands several times for inflated transfer fees. One of his many ports of call had been Liverpool and, during his brief stay there, the unfortunate lad went down injured in the penalty area.

Bill Shankly, who had belatedly realized that this fellow was not quite up to Liverpool standards, studied the situation for a few moments from the touchline, then called out to the trainer on the field: 'Tie his legs together.'

Astounded, the trainer called back: 'There's nothing wrong with his legs, boss'.

Unmoved, Shanks called out again: 'Tie his legs together.'

A few minutes later the injured player was in the dressing-room and the bemused trainer, back on the bench, turned to Shanks and said: 'I don't know why you made me tie his legs together, boss, there was nothing wrong with them.'

'Aye, lad, I know,' Shanks replied, 'but I was afraid that he would get up again.'

Whether that story is true, or just part of Merseyside folklore, hardly matters. It does show something of the troubled state of soccer at the time.

One very worthwhile change in the game, in my opinion, has been the introduction of substitutes, though even that sensible move initially produced chaos because of the way it was introduced.

The overwhelming case for substitutes came in the 1957 FA Cup final between Manchester United and Aston Villa. United had already won the First Division championship by a massive eleven-point margin – and that in the days of two points for a win. They were odds-on favourites to become the first team this century to complete the League and Cup double, but the game was only a few minutes old when their goalkeeper, Ray Wood, was stretchered off after a collision with Villa's Peter McParland. United were obliged to play the rest of the match reduced to ten men with their centre-half, Jackie Blanchflower, playing in goal. They lost the match 2–1 and the final irony was that both Villa's goals were scored by McParland who, a lot of people thought, was lucky to have been allowed to stay on the pitch.

Eventually, the football authorities took the revolutionary step of allowing substitutes but, to begin with, the rules stated that substitutes could only be used to replace an injured player, which was of course a recipe for all kinds of nonsense. Except in extreme cases, how could a referee tell whether or not a player was genuinely injured? So, while in the first few weeks the clubs, grateful that the rule had been introduced, tried to live up to its spirit, there were many who started to see more interesting possibilities.

It wasn't long before every team had cottoned on to the idea of replacing an 'injured' player towards the end of the game. Twenty minutes from time seemed to be the most popular moment, and so it was that at 4.20 on a typical Saturday afternoon there was the bizarre spectacle of fully fit players being either carried off or helped off football fields all over the country. It did not take long, fortunately, for common sense to assert itself; the rule was changed and from then on substitutions could be made at the managers' discretion.

Gear change

Footballers became fashion trendsetters in the mid-Sixties as the modern player went through a process of emancipation, turning from serf into socialite. The effects of the abolition of the maximum wage, in 1961, had begun to give players a sense of financial security; then my old colleague George Best set a completely new tone by opening a boutique – a type of shop which was itself a new phenomenon at the time – and appearing on the covers, not only of sports papers but fashion magazines as well. Suddenly, we were in the age of the fashion-conscious footballer. Carnaby Street had come into the game and once-humble soccer players were acquiring the status of film stars.

In the matter of hairstyles Derek Dougan, then with Blackburn Rovers, was way ahead of his time when he appeared in the 1960 FA Cup final, against Wolves, with his head completely shaved. Most players were travelling in the opposite direction, and shoulder-length barnets were soon entirely normal.

Saturday afternoon at the average football ground saw a parade of hairstyles which would not have looked out of place in a chorus line. On a practical level, the extra couple of inches of lacquered blow-wave could be all-important in a heading duel – though spiky styles were not favoured in case the ball got burst.

The new hairstyles also brought with them problems of identification. When George Best decided to adopt a Beatles mop, half the young players in the game did the same. A decade later the Afro look was all the rage and our football fields were full of Afro lookalikes, the vast majority of them recognizable only by the number on their back.

My own hairstyle was one of the most distinctive in the game, but it didn't come out of a hairdressing salon. It was just the natural result of sweeping my blond locks back with a comb. Rod Stewart paid me the compliment of having his hair fashioned to look like mine as part of his conversion from Cockney to pseudo-Scot.

Kit began to change when the sportswear industry became competitive. The old brown leather boots were quickly phased out in favour of black and white patterned lightweight models, a development which led to a certain amount of skullduggery. Leading players signed contracts with manufacturers to sponsor particular boots. The trouble was, they didn't always want to wear the boots

29

they were sponsoring. This led to some ridiculous compromises, with the player painting on imitation trademarks so that he could continue wearing his favourite boots while appearing to sponsor another brand.

On one occasion a club manager did a deal for his whole team to wear a brand new set of boots in a Cup final. The players, however, preferred the boots of another manufacturer. The difference between the two models was that the ones the players were already wearing, and preferred, had a series of white stripes running down the side. Otherwise, the two sets of boots looked identical. The players' solution was to pull-off the tell-tale white stripes. Unfortunately, anyone looking closely could easily see the marks where the white stripes had been.

Shirts and shorts also underwent a transformation. Shirts became neater and tighter, and shorts have gone from brief to ultra-brief. Team colours may now change regularly, usually to incorporate a manufacturer's logo or style – a trend which seemed to gain official approval in the early Seventies when Don Revie, then

England's team manager, signed a contract with Admiral and abandoned the traditional black and white national strip in favour of the now familiar red, white and blue pyjama tops. Well, do you know anybody who likes them?

The latest innovation is advertising on shirts, providing a source of revenue which football in its present economic plight no doubt urgently needs. I wonder, though, if this development had taken place in the days of my childhood, just after the war – would we have seen players wearing sandwich boards?

ON MANOEUVRES

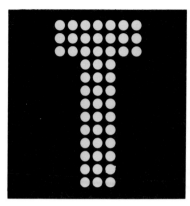actics in soccer are just like military ploys, aimed at bringing down the enemy. Pushing, shirt-tugging and the straightforward trip are the game's most basic tactical manoeuvres. More subtle variations include ankle-tapping, stealing ground at throw-ins and free-kicks, and grabbing an opponent by the hand to prevent him from getting away. These, though, are mere trifles compared with some of the things which go unnoticed.

An unwritten rule of the tactical game is that wherever possible the offended party must get his own back in some subtle way, and sometimes the duel is carried over from one game to another. A certain well-known international centre-forward was renowned for using elbows, fists and sometimes even his head in those close encounters which so often occur in the goalmouth. A couple of seasons ago he 'clobbered' an opposing goalkeeper late in the game and the

offended 'keeper had no opportunity to take his revenge that afternoon. But, just like the elephant, the goalkeeper didn't forget. The season progressed and in due course the two teams were scheduled to meet again.

Before the start of the return match the goalkeeper, who was also a well-known international, was heard to mutter darkly: 'I'll have that bastard before the afternoon is out.' Those of us who were in the know settled back in the stands to watch the match wondering how he would work it. Anyone can punch an opponent on the nose; the trick is to get away with it.

More than seventy minutes of the match had gone, when a long ball pumped out of defence saw the centre-forward chasing into the penalty area. The goalkeeper, noting that the referee was miles behind the play, came off his line like a flash. As the ball bounced, the two men closed on their collision course, and rose in the air together. At the moment of impact, the goalkeeper's right knee came up and caught the centre-forward full in the gut. The two men fell in a heap.

Now came the subtle bit. With his adversary writhing on the ground, the goalkeeper raised his left arm in a gesture of self-blame and knelt beside the stricken warrior, feigning concern. 'Honours' were even.

Diving practice

There is a very special art to diving. Top men can go down so dramatically that the average referee is bound to give a free-kick, and if the 'offence' happened to take place inside the penalty area, so much the better.

When Malcolm Allison was in his first spell as manager of Manchester City, there were rumours around the town that he had Francis Lee practising his tumbles inside the penalty area. At the time Franny had the nickname 'Lee Won Pen' in Manchester, and with his short legs and tubby build he certainly had the ideal diver's body. Far be it from me to say that the rumours were true, but there was one season during that period when he was awarded somewhere in the region of a dozen penalties.

There are certain grounds where it is known to be dangerous to tackle a home forward inside the penalty area. The spontaneous reaction of the crowd

The **Sun** 3p

LEE WINS LAST MINUTE PENALTY

can influence a referee, who may not be totally sure of what he has seen. Thirty-odd thousand voices howling 'Penalty' can be a very persuasive force. The Anfield Kop is the classic example.

When Swansea played there, in their first season in the First
Division, the match ended in a 2–2 draw, both Liverpool's goals
coming from penalties awarded in front of the Kop. After the match
the Swansea manager, John Toshack, himself a former Anfield idol,
was heard to remark, ruefully: 'I told my lads to watch what they
were doing inside that penalty area.'

Delaying tactics are basically negative, but can be highly
effective. They range from holding on to the ball, or taking time over
goal-kicks and corners, to refusing to stay more than ten yards away
from the ball at a free-kick. This forces the referee to keep pushing
the wall back and pacing out the ten yards over and over again.

A favourite delaying tactic of the Spanish and Portuguese,
among others, is the 'dying swan act'. This ruse normally comes into

play when the opposing team is playing particularly well; in fact the idea is to break up their rhythm. Constant stoppages in play make it difficult for a team to keep up its momentum. So, whenever a Spanish or Portuguese team is under pressure, it comes as no great surprise to see their players begin to drop like ninepins all over the field. The moment they get within two feet of a tackle, down they go, as if shot, and begin the familiar rolling-around-in-agony routine.

The 'injured' player then makes an incredibly quick recovery and can often be seen, a couple of minutes later, sprinting the length of the field and even firing in a fierce shot with the leg which a few moments earlier he appeared to think was broken.

Strikes, Italian style

For sheer cynicism, though, it takes a lot to beat the Italians. I had a whole season of learning about their off-the-ball tactics, and I still carry some of the scars. In Italy, everything is about timing – knowing the moment to 'strike'.

Imagine that one side has won a corner-kick and players of both sides are crowded in the penalty area. The moment for the defending side to 'strike' is the instant the kick is taken. The ball will be in the air and, all being well, the referee's eyes will be on it. Down below, in the turmoil around the penalty spot, elbows are going into ribs, punches are being thrown and defenders are levering themselves up on the shoulders of their opponents to gain extra height. If there is any doubt about who did what and to whom, the referee will generally adopt a safety-first policy of giving a free-kick to the defending side.

Revenge takes the form of a 'commando raid', which occurs

when play has moved to the opposite end of the field. The offended forward waits until he is sure that the referee and linesmen are looking the other way, then makes a quick 'strike' against his opposite number and quickly sprints to another part of the field. By the time the referee is aware that something has happened, all he can see is a prostrate figure on the ground but no opposing player within thirty yards.

The South Americans can be even more fiendish, something I learned at first hand when Manchester United met Estudiantes of Argentina in the World Club Championship, in 1969. The tactical battle began when we arrived at our accommodation. The Hindu Club, where we stayed, is a high-class establishment situated about twenty miles out of the centre of Buenos Aires.

The day we arrived, the lifts suddenly all went out of service, which was no joke since our rooms were spread out between the tenth and fifteenth floors. This meant that we had a long haul upstairs every time we needed to go to our rooms – and heaven help the man who got down to the ground floor and then found that he had left something important behind. Coincidences do occur, of course, but it seemed to us more than a coincidence that the lifts were mysteriously working again the morning after we had lost the match 1–0.

The night before the game we were invited to a reception in the centre of Buenos Aires, where we were supposed to meet and socialize with our opponents. A forty-mile round trip through the busy streets of the capital was not the preparation Matt Busby would normally have chosen on the eve of a match, but being always conscious of public relations and not wishing to offend our hosts he agreed that we would attend. What he had not bargained for was that not a single Estudiantes player would turn up. We were furious but just had to grin and bear it.

In the match itself, there were even harder lessons to be learned about the South American way of football. One of the hardest was what might be called the 'double-bluff' foul. This begins with an opponent running into you and knocking you to the ground. He then throws up his hands in that all-too-familiar plea of innocence which seems to fool most Latin referees. Then, to prove that he's really a nice chap and means no harm, he puts his arm around you and helps you back to your feet. What the referee doesn't know is that as he is helping you up he's either pinching the tender flesh under your armpit or pulling your hair. When your instinctive reaction is to push him away, you appear to be the bad guy.

In fact, if he was really on song, that kind of opponent could a) win a free-kick, b) injure you and c) get you sent off. That's tactics!

THE RULING CLASSES

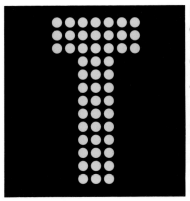

The disciplinary hearing is football's equivalent of a magistrates' court. Players who have been sent off, or collected sufficient bookings, appear before them to be tried and sentenced. Today it's a fairly straightforward procedure, with set penalties for most offences, and players are allowed to be properly represented, calling witnesses and producing televised evidence in their defence, if they want to. It wasn't always so civilized.

The first of a number of appearances I made before the court was in November 1963. At that time the player 'on trial' was not allowed to speak. He was represented by the PFA secretary, Cliff Lloyd, who did his best, but the odds were stacked against him. The hearing took place in Sheffield and we were ushered into a room where four or five of the game's leading administrators were seated around a large oak table. The proceedings had the flavour of a cut-and-dried affair. I was charged with having been involved in a brawl, at Villa Park, and it came as no surprise when I was found guilty. What was a surprise was the severity of the punishment: a

THE CARPET

twenty-eight day suspension. That meant one month's loss of earnings. The only consolation was that, because I was suspended through Christmas and the New Year, I could spend the festive season with my family in Aberdeen. The trouble was, there would be no money to buy presents.

Ironically, almost exactly twelve months later I was 'on trial' again, but by now conditions had improved a little. I was able to call a witness, Pat Crerand, and put forward a bit of a defence. I was accused of using a four-letter word to the referee during a match at Blackpool. My defence was that I had been misheard. The word I had actually used was 'coot' and it had not been addressed to the referee but to my colleague Pat Crerand. Of course, the ruse was transparently thin and once again I was found guilty. Meanwhile, though, I could not help noticing that all through the proceedings one of the great men who was sitting in judgment on me was fast asleep.

When the chairman of the hearing eventually asked the slumbering 'juror' for his views, he spluttered into life and replied: 'I agree entirely, sir.' The outcome for me was another twenty-eight day suspension, plus a £50 fine. Once again I was bound for Aberdeen at Christmas – a coincidence spotted by quite a few people who also jumped to the unlikely conclusion that I had done it deliberately. I'll admit that the idea of having another Christmas at

I would think, the best games are the ones where the ref is not noticed --- I haven't as yet refereed in one!

home appealed to me, but does anyone know a Scot who would give up £1,000 in wages (by today's standards more like £5,000) just so that he could go home for Christmas?

There was a rather unhappy sequel to that hearing when, a few years later, my wife and I were on holiday in Spain and I bumped into the same referee in the toilet at Barcelona airport. He boasted to me that he had made £7,000 out of stories he had given to the newspapers about the incident with me, and another involving Malcolm Allison. The idea of him making all that money at my expense completely ruined my holiday.

Trial by video

Television came to the aid of a number of players who had been wrongly or mistakenly accused and it came to mine after I had been booked, in a match at Derby, for refusing to stand ten yards away from the ball at a free-kick. At the hearing, the referee repeated his charge that 'Law refused to stand ten yards away from the ball.' Luckily for me, the match had been televised and my television evidence revealed that when the referee booked me he was holding the ball underneath his arm. Case dismissed!

The chairman of the hearing was the former Burnley chairman, Bob Lord, who was clearly unhappy that I was getting off. He looked at the video recording several times and eventually spotted Bobby Charlton apparently kicking the ball away from a free-kick. 'Look at that,' he said, 'Bobby Charlton should have been booked.' Talk about clutching at straws.

One effect television has had on the game is to turn referees into personalities. You must have seen them. There's the one who runs backwards; the one who does the knees-up run; the one with the strange crouching run; the one who trots along with one arm up in the air and so on. That last trick is quite difficult to do, in fact, and needs a lot of practice. It's well beyond the brainpower of some refs, who would certainly fall over if they tried it! Probably swallow their whistle as well.

I've always believed that the best referee is the one you don't notice. If you can't remember the referee's name at the end of the match it generally means that he's had a good game. It is the same in boxing: there are always three men in the ring, but you rarely notice more than two of them.

Obviously not everyone agrees with that point of view. Recently I heard Clive Thomas in a television interview saying that fifteen years ago he thought that people came to matches to see him. Now, fifteen years later, he was certain that they did. Whether that's true or not, there's little doubt that television has turned a number of referees into actors who miss no opportunity to grab the headlines. Clive sometimes appears to be one of them.

I can't think of anyone else who would have disallowed the equalizing 'goal' scored by Brazil, against Sweden, in the 1978 World Cup. The ball went into the net direct from a corner-kick. Clive allowed the kick to be taken, then blew his whistle for half-time while the ball was in flight. That was some split-second decision. Fortunately for Clive, Brazil did score another goal in the second half – otherwise, the way those South Americans can react, we might never have seen him again.

I often wonder what goes through the mind of a faint-hearted official in some of the more volatile countries. 'Will my car be there after the match?' 'Will I still get my fee if I give the away team a penalty?' 'If I need a police escort, how do I know whose side they're on?'

TRIBAL INSTINCTS

omewhere in Liverpool there is a young man with eleven Christian names: one for each of the eleven players who made up the Liverpool first team on the day he was born. That lad's father could hardly have made a more dramatic statement of his 'faith'. God knows what his wife thought, or what he would have done if the unthinkable had happened and the lad turned into an Evertonian!

Merseyside is, of course, one of those remarkable areas where, for a large section of the community, football is a way of life: a place where commitment to a team can be a whole lot more binding than a marriage contract, and the fortunes of the club affect the fan's entire outlook and behaviour from one match day to the next.

Psychologists have suggested that this fanatical loyalty to a football club is an echo of some basic instinct buried deep in man's soul, a sort of modern-day tribalism. Where once men wore feathers in their hair and painted their faces, now they wear coloured scarves and hats to indicate their allegiance. The behaviour of football fans the world over is riddled with evidence to support this 'tribal' theory.

Different nationalities choose different methods of demonstrating their support for their team. Whistles and drums are very popular on the European continent, although the Germans are particularly fond of the hunting horn. The noise can be pretty distracting if you're not used to it.

Firework displays are all the rage in a lot of South American countries, and when Uruguay scored the winning goal of the 1980 Gold Cup final, against Brazil, the fireworks were acccompanied by the spectacle of the whole Uruguayan team jumping into the moat which surrounded the pitch. Imagine a British team doing that on a cold Saturday in January.

The Argentines greet their team, or a goal, with a spectacular 'snowstorm' of paper – a New World variation on the toilet-roll theme so popular in England. But, for my money, the most colourful of the lot are the Brazilians. Wherever Brazil play, in whatever part of the world, they are followed by thousands of yellow and green decked supporters and the focal point of their support is the fabulous Samba band, which beats out a relentless rhythm throughout the match. You can't get much more tribal than that.

Something which never ceases to amaze me is the way in which the great British terrace choirs appear to think with a collective mind. A chant or a chorus can be spontaneously improvised by ten thousand voices, each in some mystical way seeming to know the exact words and the tune that goes with them.

One of the big recent successes of television drama was the BBC series *Boys from the Blackstuff*. The stories were set on Merseyside and one of the central characters, Yosser Hughes, going out of his head because he couldn't get a job, repeatedly used the phrase, 'I can do that'. While the series was being screened, I was at Anfield and saw Sammy Lee take a corner-kick in front of the Kop. He sliced the kick badly and the ball had scarcely disappeared into the crowd before the whole Kop chorused in one voice: 'I can do that'.

On another occasion, Luton were the visitors to Anfield and during the match their goalkeeper, Findlay, was injured and had to leave the field. He was replaced between the posts by Stephens, who had barely taken up his position before the whole Kop was singing, to the tune *Guantanomera* 'There's only one Shakin' Stevens'. After Liverpool had scored a couple of goals, the chant changed to a teasing 'Stephens for England'. No wonder some visitors to Anfield get the idea they're a goal down before they've even run out on the pitch!

In the land of the Godfather

One group of supporters who could well do with an injection of the Kop's sense of good humour are the Italians. The most cheerless place on earth to play football must be Sicily, where the atmosphere at a match is always ugly and can be frightening. Visiting teams are not expected to win there.

Long before
the debate about fencing-
in the crowds came to Britain, Sicilian
fans were caged up like wild animals behind
high-wire fences, which was a visiting player's sole guarantee of
safety. I still have bad dreams remembering that sea of snarling faces
spitting at me through the wire and I can well understand why the
great Sivori, who played for Juventus in the Sixties, refused to
appear there.

Nor were the crowds further north particularly angelic.
Whenever we played in Venice, the trip to the ground had to be
made by gondola along the city's canal system. At various points
along the way there are bridges and it was, and is, not unknown for
supporters of the home team to lie in wait and empty their dustbins
onto the visiting team's transport.

On one occasion, in my Torino days, Joe Baker and I were
involved in a scuffle with a persistent Venetian photographer which
came to an unpopular conclusion when Joe knocked the man
down. This episode, which happened before the match, inflamed the
local fans and, after we had made matters worse by taking a point
from the game, our journey back to our hotel turned into a running
siege. It wasn't just rubbish that came down on us that night, but
rocks, bottles and lumps of wood. It was a miracle no-one was hurt.

In the very early days of European competition, British clubs learned about another little ruse, popular in both Italy and Spain, which was calculated to upset visiting teams. An army of local fans would station themselves outside the team's hotel and keep them awake all night sounding car horns and beating drums. Whatever happened to the idea that it is 'the game that matters'?

Tartan fandango

One of the great footballing hordes was Scotland's own Tartan Army, 1978 vintage, which travelled to Argentina for the World Cup. Literally thousands of them hitch-hiked halfway across the world, travelling through as many as a dozen different countries, being arrested and robbed in every town they came to, only to see their football dreams crushed in little more than a week. They deserved a gold medal.

I spoke to one who had set off from Scotland more than three months before the finals were due to be played. He had flown to the United States, then hitch-hiked down, crossing the Panama Canal and travelling through Colombia, Ecuador, Peru and Bolivia before entering Chile and crossing the Andes to Argentina.

By the time the Scotland team arrived in Cordoba, hundreds of supporters were waiting there for them. They were greeted by a pipe band and a civic reception staged by the local townspeople, who seemed to find something they liked in the Scottish character. It was a wild night, a fitting sequel to the build-up which had begun at Hampden Park during the last match of the home international championship. Afterwards, the team had travelled by motorcade direct to the airport, and were given a tremendous send-off. The fact that they had just been defeated by England – in ordinary circumstances a national disaster – hardly seemed to matter. Scotland's manager, Ally McLeod, had been built up by the Scottish press – and others who should have known better – into a sort of footballing Pied Piper who, it was confidently expected, would lead the Tartan horde to fresh fields of conquest and greater glory in Argentina. No-one foresaw that the new Crown Prince of Scottish football was within days of being relegated to Court Jester. Four years later, in Spain, the Scottish fans were still extracting bitter pleasure from the Argentine misadventure, encouraging their team with shouts of 'Don't worry, lads, Ally's back in Scotland.' It can be a cruel game as well as a funny one.

Argie-bargie

If Scotland's World Cup was to turn sour in 1978, not so Argentina's. I was in Rosario the night they beat Peru 6–0 in the final match of the second group stage – a result which gave them a place in the World Cup final ahead of their old enemy, Brazil. Let no-one run away with the idea that Peru either threw that match or were a pushover. They were simply swept aside on a wave of national fervour by an Argentine side which knew that it had to win by four clear goals to go through.

After the match, I flew back to Buenos Aires with a group of radio and television colleagues. When we arrived at the airport, we discovered that our flight was also carrying a large contingent of ecstatic Argentine fans. The flight took a couple of hours and all the way the fans were singing and dancing in the narrow aisle, creating scenes I could never have imagined on an aircraft. They even had me starting to forget my flight nerves. I have a habit in the few moments before take-off and landing of closing my eyes. Most people think I'm asleep, but those who know me well know that I'm not sleeping, I'm praying!

As we flew over Buenos Aires it was a beautifully clear evening and we had a good view of everything on the ground. We came in low over the River Plate and suddenly the stadium was below us; it was fully lit and the newly painted structure looked magnificent, with its steeply tiered seating and high sides, for all the world like a modern Colosseum.

The pilot was giving a running commentary on the scene below. It was more like a coach tour than a flight. The Argentine punters had no interest in sitting down and fastening their seat belts, they were still dancing in the aisle. On the ground we could see the motorcades blocking the main streets and we could almost hear the carnival which we knew was going on down there. We reached about treetop height, and could see the people in the streets, as the plane glided down towards the runway. Then, suddenly, there was a dramatic roar as the aircraft's engines burst back into life. In an instant we were roaring back up into the sky instead of gliding down. My head shot between my knees. 'Jesus Christ,' I said. 'We're going down.' All my fears came rushing back in those seconds; I thought it was the end.

Instead, the aircraft continued to gain height steadily, flew once around the airfield and came down again, this time to a perfectly smooth landing. As we taxied across the tarmac I realized that throughout the whole drama the Argentine fans had never broken their routine of singing and dancing. They either hadn't known what had happened or just didn't care.

The official explanation, offered to us by a smiling cabin steward, was that we had been caught by a cross-wind and had to abort. I will always believe that the pilot was so busy doing his commentary that he simply missed the runway. Either way, it did little to improve my enthusiasm for flying. No wonder they say that

Argentine airlines have difficulty getting insurance cover!

Back on earth, we found that the roads between the airport and our hotel were jammed solid, and it was virtually impossible to move in the direction we wanted to go. After a while our driver hit on a novel solution. He crossed the central reservation and began heading into town along the opposite carriageway, which was comparatively clear. At one point we met a truck coming in the opposite direction at a hell of a speed. Neither our driver nor the truck driver seemed prepared to give way until they were almost on top of one another. Then, at the last moment, they both swerved outwards and we flashed past with a babble of Spanish oaths hanging on the night air. So that's what they mean by a Mexican stand-off.

The celebrations went on all through the night. Sleep was out of the question. Our hotel was on one of the capital's main streets and even double-glazed windows could not keep out the noise of the street bands down below.

The Siege of Wembley

Every group of supporters has its own way of celebrating and sometimes the celebrations get a bit out of hand. A few seasons ago, Scotland beat England at Wembley and the overjoyed fans ran onto the pitch and carried off pieces of goalpost and lumps of turf for souvenirs. This didn't go down too well with the authorities, of course, and two years later anyone wearing tartan was lucky to get an orange juice in London's West End. No doubt the fans shouldn't have done some of the things they did, but even that infamous day had its funny side. I remember leaving Wembley an hour or so after the match and seeing half-a-dozen Scots carrying a huge length of crossbar down into the Underground. I couldn't help wondering how the hell they were going to get it onto the train and back up to Scotland.

For a couple of weeks after that match, clumps of 'genuine Wembley turf' were on sale all over Glasgow. I heard that one man made a small fortune after investing in some whitewash and turf; his line was in 'genuine Wembley penalty spots'.

One of my first visits to Wembley as a member of the ITV commentary team was for a match between England and Scotland. It was a very warm, sunny afternoon and after the match the terraces at the end where the Scottish supporters had been standing were wet through from top to bottom. I remember wondering to myself: 'Where did all that water come from?' Then it dawned on me that during the afternoon a few shandies had been drunk and later, like water, had found their own level. No Scot ever wants to miss a moment of the action.

Carry-on at Crewe

Perhaps the one characteristic which football fans the world over have in common is their eternal optimism. In February 1960, Tottenham Hotspur were on the verge of producing perhaps the best team in the club's history. Their line-up included such notables as Danny Blanchflower, Dave Mackay, John White, and a host of other international players. They were, undoubtedly, one of the most powerful teams in the land.

The fourth round of the FA Cup had brought them an away tie against Fourth Division Crewe Alexandra. It should have been a walkover, but cup ties can produce unexpected results. Crewe almost pulled off what would have been the shock of the season; they led 2–1 until Spurs equalized late in the game to earn a replay at White Hart Lane. Having had one narrow escape, Spurs could hardly be expected to let a second opportunity slip, and on their own ground, and sure enough the replay was a massacre. They scored ten goals in the first half and eventually won the match 13–2.

That evening, the Crewe secretary had stayed at his office sorting out some of the mass of paperwork which the two matches had generated. As he and a couple of colleagues worked, they kept in touch with the progress of the match at White Hart Lane by telephone. Throughout the evening, they themselves received phone calls from their own supporters, wanting to know the latest score.

Shortly before half-time, one hopeful character rang and inquired: 'What's the score at White Hart Lane?'

'Seven nil,' the secretary replied, and was about to put down the receiver when the voice inquired again: 'Who to?'

THE INNER SANCTUM

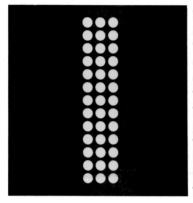

t is a cold November evening, damp and slightly misty. Somewhere out in the gloom twenty-two young men are chasing a ball about the field in an earnest attempt to play football. The feeble yellowish rays of the stadium floodlights cast shadows on the grassless pitch. In the darkness, on the terraces, the long-suffering supporters huddle together in small groups, hands in pockets, vainly stamping their feet for warmth.

Under the main stand a single yellow light stands out like a small beacon, indicating the location of the press box. Here, a handful of reporters, most of them young fresh-faced lads learning their trade, some older, seeing out the years before retirement, wait patiently for the half-time whistle – the signal to phone over first-half copy.

To the right of the press box is an enclosure with seating slightly plusher than elsewhere: the directors' box. Here sit a group of middle-aged men buttoned up in large black overcoats, tartan car rugs wrapped around their legs to keep out the chill night air; also a woman wrapped in a fur coat, trying to look interested, but seeming distinctly uncomfortable. On the front row a visiting manager, an honoured guest wearing only a thin raincoat, steels himself against the winter chill and waits for half-time and the reward of a whisky and hot water. Such is life in the Fourth Division.

Relief at last. The whistle blows and the battle-weary warriors troop off the field, heads down, away for their half-time orange and a quick pep talk. The faithful few shuffle off in search of hot Bovril and a pork pie; the pressmen begin to dial; the elderly gents in their Crombies move off with their solitary guest and the forlorn lady, indoors to the directors' guest room, where wait the tea ladies with their china cups and plates of sandwiches – and beyond them the inner sanctum of the directors' bar and more manly refreshments.

Soon, the half-time formalities over, the match restarts. There is no appreciable improvement in the quality of the play. Gradually boredom and disillusionment begin to affect the small throng of ever-hopefuls. They had expected at least a home win, but so far no goals have been scored.

The focus of attention is shifting away from the field of play towards that privileged area in the centre of the stand. A small crowd is gathering in front of the men who rule. Now backs are turned towards the play, a new source of entertainment has been found. It's 'bait the officials' time.

The visiting manager has been the object of banter and mild abuse right from the start. Now the chairman and his board are in the firing line. The night air rings with taunts and catcalls, some of it good-natured, some with a cutting edge. 'What a load of rubbish!' 'When are we going to buy some decent players?' 'Look at them, straight out of Madame Tussaud's.' There is a peal of laughter and one or two of the overcoats twitch, as the wearer's embarrassment grows. Meanwhile, the twenty-two young men continue to chase the ball around in the gloom, unnoticed in the background.

Eventually, sweet release – the final whistle. Now the frozen few trudge homeward darkly muttering their discontent, questioning the wisdom of having come, vowing not to come again. In the press box, the young wordsmiths struggle to create a story with shape and meaning out of the featureless muddle they have just witnessed.

In the warmth of the inner sanctum, the chairman stands with his back to the electric fire. He stops dramatically in the act of pouring a large whisky for one of the guests, the glass still held in his

51

left hand, the whisky decanter in his right. Affecting the manner of someone making an important announcement he speaks:

'I can take their insults,' he says. 'I can take their poison-pen letters and their abusive phone calls.' He throws his arms wide in an expansive gesture, still holding the glass and decanter. 'But *this* is what it's all about – my friends.'

Everyone drinks to that.

TEAM MATES

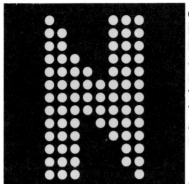

obby Stiles made his début for England in 1965, against Scotland at Wembley. I know, because I was the man in the Scotland team that Nobby was set to mark. He and I were Manchester United team-mates at the time, and quite good friends, but all that would have to be set aside for the ancient duel of the two nations.

But 'Happy', as we had nicknamed him at Old Trafford, apparently didn't realize the significance of the event, and as the teams were lining up in the tunnel, shortly before the kick-off, he caught my eye and called across: 'Hi Denis – good luck'.

Instead of replying, I just looked straight through him, then turned away. He must have wondered what the hell was going on. It turned out to be the worst thing I could have done, because Happy then spent the rest of the afternoon kicking me from one end of Wembley to the other.

Few players made a greater impact (no pun intended) than Nobby in the Sixties, but his reputation for being a tough guy was largely a myth. The real problem was that he couldn't see properly. He wore very thick contact lenses, and it was quite an operation in the dressing-room before matches to get them fitted. He used to struggle with them for hours. Even when he had successfully slotted them in, his vision was only slightly improved. The result was that he was always several inches out with his tackling: a tackle aimed around the ankle could easily end up around the knee, and a knee-high tackle generally landed on the hip. No wonder the Argentine press labelled him 'El Bandito'. Another so-called 'hard man' in the Old Trafford squad was Maurice Setters. Built like a brick privvy and sporting a close - cropped hairstyle, Maurice looked a lot fiercer than he was. What he certainly was,

was bow-legged: he should have had an entry in the *Guinness Book of Records* – the only man who could be nutmegged from eighty yards.

The real tough guy in the United side was Bill Foulkes, who was immune to pain. He started life as a full-back, but eventually became the regular centre-half after the Munich air disaster. Bill was a centre-half in the traditional mould, used to taking on a strong bustling centre-forward. He wasn't too happy against small, lively forwards like Joe Baker or Ian St John, who could lead him a dance, but put him against someone like Tony Hately or Andy Lockhead and he was in his element. You could always tell a centre-forward who had played against Bill by the big knee impression in his back and the elbow imprint on his head.

Centre-half and centre-forward are two of the three positions for which I have always thought one of the prime qualifications was to be a little bit round the bend. The other was goalkeeper and no-one fitted that particular bill better than Harry Gregg.

Harry was a hero of Munich and as good a goalkeeper as there was around at the time. He was as brave as a lion, but also as mad as a hatter. I remember once we were playing Blackburn Rovers in a First Division match (that had to be a long time ago). The ball came across from the wing into United's penalty area and there was a mêlée, with Harry buried somewhere in the middle of it. All of a sudden, Ferguson, the Blackburn inside-forward, let out a scream: 'The bastard's bit me,' he cried, and, sure enough, there were the teeth marks on his thigh where Harry had tried to take a piece out of him.

Another who was slightly round the bend was our Republic of Ireland full-back, Noel Cantwell. True to his Irish ancestry 'The Professor', as some of the lads used to call him, had really kissed the Blarney stone; which was why he was eventually made club captain.

Noel joined us from West Ham and for a time was captain on the field. Then he lost his place in the first team and I was made captain. But I wasn't too keen on the public relations side of the job. Someone had to act as the players' spokesman and Noel was the ideal choice. So he was made non-playing club captain, and, while I did the graft on the field, he did all the talking off it.

The two full-back roles had been taken over by those two other Republic of Ireland stalwarts, Shay Brennan and Tony Dunne. Tony had the reputation of being the fastest full-back of the day, and he was also one of the first to play the overlap. He was very effective at making a run the length of the field and getting himself up into an attacking right-wing position. The trouble was that he couldn't cross the ball accurately. If our forwards had been allowed to go into the crowd behind the goal to meet Tony's crosses, things would have been a lot better.

On the subject of crosses, no-one I ever played with had better control of a cross than my old mate Paddy Crerand. Paddy was a really stylish player whose pace was deceptive. His quick brain and accurate eye made up for the fact that he was basically slow. I used to say that he was a boon to television in the days before the action replay. With Paddy it wasn't necessary to slow the action down to see what had happened; slow-motion was his natural speed.

Our most elegant player was David Sadler, a good all-round sportsman. He was good at golf and could have played cricket for Kent. He gave up a job in a bank to come to Old Trafford and had the unusual distinction of playing both centre-half and centre-forward for us at different times. He was a real jack of all trades, but unfortunately not quite master of any.

Once we were playing Everton in the Charity Shield match, at Goodison Park. We were getting hammered, 4–0, when we won a corner and David went over to take it. He placed the ball then stepped back to weigh up the situation in the penalty area. Unfortunately, when he took the kick he missed the ball and lifted the flag out of the ground. It just about summed up the kind of day we were having.

One man who could certainly not be called elegant was our regular centre-forward, David Herd. David – the gentle giant – moved as if he had two left feet, but no-one could hit a ball harder. On one occasion a machine was brought to Old Trafford to measure the velocity of shots. David was clocked at almost eighty miles an hour. I remember a match against Sunderland in which they used three different goalkeepers. The first two had to be taken off injured trying to save shots from David's lethal right boot.

That lethal *left* boot, Bobby Charlton, once laid out a referee with an off-target effort which rebounded into the net. The unconscious referee was unable to say that a genuine goal had been scored and had to order a bounce-up at the spot where he had been flattened.

It wasn't very often that Bobby scored with a header, but that was how he scored his most important goal for United. I'm not sure he knew much about it, but he aimed that shiny dome at a crossed ball and saw it glide off into the corner of Benfica's net, during the 1968 European Cup Final. I've often thought that if Bobby had had any hair, the ball would probably have gone over the bar.

The wayward genius of Old Trafford was my old friend Georgie Best. George the enigma: almost the best player I ever saw, except for his tendency to hold onto the ball when he should have passed to someone in a better position. But how many times did he hold onto it and, just when you were cursing him, the ball was flying into the back of the net?

George was a simple lad at heart who just loved playing football. He would have been happy if he could have played all eleven positions himself. His great talent produced enormous pressures, about which others can speculate, but only he will ever really know. Surely, though, few players ever gave the fans greater entertainment.

THE PRESS GANG

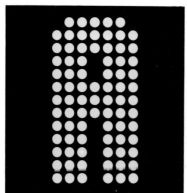 young player who had made a fairly dramatic impact on the game, having been capped at the age of eighteen and enjoyed a couple of seasons in the headlines, was approached by a local newspaper reporter. Since his international début, he had progressed from the Second Division club, where he had started his footballing career, to one of the biggest clubs in the country. Unfortunately, the big club were now perilously close to the bottom of the First Division and in great danger of being relegated.

The reporter's first question was: 'If City go down, will you be prepared to go back to the Second Division?'

The lad replied to the effect that he didn't really fancy returning to the Second Division. After all, he had just begun to make his name at international level and it would obviously be better for his career if he could stay in the First.

The next day the local paper carried a banner headline on its sportspage: LAW SAYS: 'IF CITY GO DOWN, I LEAVE'. The news was as welcome in Manchester as a lead brick through the front-room window.

The experience taught me an important lesson. Newspapermen can be great guys and may even be your friends, but you have to be careful what you say to them. I suppose it can be argued that the headline had reflected the implication of what I had said the previous day. What it certainly didn't convey was the spirit in which I had said it.

Football and the press enjoy a love-hate relationship. Reporters want stories which will attract readers and the vast majority of clubs badly want the publicity. But they can't always agree on what should be published, or when. Some clubs would like to dictate to the newspapers which stories they should print and which they should not. The sensible ones learn to live with the press, using it whenever they can but accepting that not all that is written will be to their liking.

Tinker, tailor, soldier . . . footballer

The biggest football stories are usually about players being transferred. However, it is often in the purchasing club's interest for such deals to be conducted in secrecy. Once a player has been signed they will gladly call a press conference where everyone is welcome to share controlled information. What often precedes these events is a bizarre cat-and-mouse game which would not be out of place in a detective novel. For while the manager buying a player usually wants to act with speed and discretion, the manager selling may very likely try to attract alternative bidders in the hope of upping the price, so he may be prepared to leak a discreet word to a friendly reporter.

There may also be more than one player involved in the deal, and perhaps one of the 'makeweights' is unhappy with his treatment. Other problems face the player who wants a move but is contractually unable to ask for a transfer; and the manager who would like to invite offers for a contracted player but cannot go on the open market and say so. Either is quite likely to feed a story to the newspapers in order to draw attention to his problem. All the while, the newspapers themselves are searching hungrily for stories.

It is fertile ground for cloak-and-dagger intrigues involving secret meetings, press leaks, the wholesale telling of half-truths and downright untruths, and for large helpings of wild speculation. Anxious to meet a deadline, the reporter takes a 'flier'. Information is assessed, two and two are added, and sometimes the result makes five. 'Bloggs signs for Spurs today'; 'Forest are ready to release

Blank'; 'United want £500,000 for Higgins'. We've all seen the headlines. Sometimes the story is on the mark, sometimes it's not. Either way it sells newspapers and seems to keep readers happy.

A good newspaperman is a tough, durable character who's able to take the rough with the smooth. The work is not so much about listening at keyholes as about building a network of reliable contacts, winning people's confidence and keeping well informed. It is not glamorous, but, to judge from the views of the hundreds of reporters I know, seems to be good fun.

The press corps, by and large, stick together. On overseas trips you don't have to look far to find them. The first port of call is the hotel bar and, apart from press briefings, team training sessions, the match itself, and brief spells in the sack, that's where they'll be for the duration, sharpening their quills and their wits.

One thing you do need to survive in this jungle is a sense of humour. A few seasons ago, while all the London teams were having a lean time, Liverpool were, as usual, sweeping everything before them, and Tommy Docherty's Manchester United were setting the world on fire with their fast exciting football. One Saturday afternoon, a large posse of the Fleet Street mafia turned up at Old Trafford. They were standing outside the dressing-room, before the match, when 'The Doc' came out of his office and saw them all standing there.

'What's the matter, isn't there a match in London today?' he asked.

Quick as a flash, one of the sages replied: 'Tom, there hasn't been a match in London for two years.'

Different newspapers have markedly different ideas about what is good for their readers. The Daily Express, for instance, has always had a tradition of being forthright and controversial. Leading columnists under the Beaverbrook banner were never afraid to express an opinion, or place their reputation on the line. When Desmond Hackett was the Express's number one football writer, he frequently backed his judgment with the outrageous statement that if Arsenal didn't beat X, or England lost to Y, 'I will eat my brown bowler'. Over the years, he had to 'eat' so many of them that I believe he eventually started to keep a supply of marzipan hats in his office.

More serious treatments can be found in a paper such as The Sunday Times, where Brian Glanville currently pens some thought-provoking pieces on the various problems of the game. The one drawback with Brian's articles is that they can be difficult to follow if you don't understand Italian.

Today there are many former players who write newspaper columns, and none is more entertaining than my old friend Danny Blanchflower. Danny has the marvellous knack of writing satirical pieces about serious subjects and making very sound points, without ever being too heavy. His adoption of the Mad Hatter and other characters from Alice in Wonderland as the cast of his 'football clinic' has created for him a unique style which is compulsive reading for thousands of Sunday Express readers.

Until his retirement, a few years ago, the doyen of the Fleet Street football brigade was Geoffrey Green of The Times. Geoffrey, who greeted everyone with the phrase 'My dear boy', was also a regular contributor to BBC Radio's Sports Report. His dark-brown velvet voice was something to look forward to on a cold winter's evening during the season. He was supremely skilful with words, offering elegance, humour and style.

A story I love concerned the occasion when Geoffrey was commissioned by the Manchester United board to write a history of the club, for publication during their centenary season. Geoffrey agreed to do this and a few months later the book proofs were sent to Old Trafford to be read and approved by the board.

On his next visit to the club Geoffrey is said to have encountered the chairman, the late Louis Edwards, and to have asked him his opinion of the manuscript. Mr Edwards replied: 'There's an awful lot in there about Matt Busby. What the hell do you think I've been doing for the past twenty years, sitting on my arse drinking champagne?'

Geoffrey apparently said, in his inimitable style: 'Frankly, old boy, yes!'

Chinese goalkeeper in Rome sex drama!

The next two stories have a common link in exaggeration. In Italy, where I played for a season, the press have few inhibitions and some journalists would jump on their grandmother's grave rather than let mere facts get in the way of a succulent story.

Torino, my team, were away to Roma, and after the match Joe

Baker and I were allowed to stay behind for a few days in the capital, which we were seeing for the first time. After a while we picked up a couple of local girls, or at least we thought we did; it turned out that they had picked us up.

The four of us went on a fairly harmless tour of a few of the city's bars and then went our separate ways. Joe and I were astonished the following day to find photographs of ourselves plastered all over the front page of one of Italy's less responsible scandal sheets. The photographer must have used an infra-red lens because we neither saw him nor even suspected his presence. Poor old Joe came out of it particularly badly; he had been caught in some innocent but embarrassing-looking poses draped over the bonnet of a car.

Later, when I was in the United States, a reporter from the Tampa Bay local paper came to talk to me about the game over there. He said that soccer's US organizers had been looking at various ways of making the game more attractive to American spectators. One of these ideas, which according to him was supported by Gordon Jago, was that the goalposts should be wider apart and the crossbar raised, thereby increasing the target area and leading to more goals being scored. What did I think?

Being something of a conservative in these matters, I said: 'No, you don't need to go to those lengths to produce more goals. Just introduce a rule that the goalkeeper must be Chinese, not more than five feet tall and have only one arm.'

The following day my 'suggestion' appeared in the local paper. I've never been quite sure whose leg was being pulled – his or mine!

The Nottingham express

A Fleet Street sports editor had been invited to take part in a sports forum at a new local radio station in Nottingham. On the day of the broadcast, he left his office very much at the last minute to catch his train. As he rushed out of the door, he instructed his new, rather dizzy, secretary to arrange for a taxi to meet him at the station in Nottingham, to take him to the broadcasting studio there.

A couple of hours later, the train pulled into Nottingham and the harassed editor charged out of the railway station, half expecting to find no taxi waiting, but he was pleasantly surprised. Hurriedly he checked that the driver was indeed waiting for him, and as he climbed into the back seat, he asked the man to take him to the radio station.

'Fine, guv,' came the reply, 'where is it?'

Puzzled, the editor repeated the question. 'Where is it? Don't *you* know?'

'No guv,' the driver replied. 'I'm not from round here, I've just been sent up from London to meet you.'

Herbie's big night

Then there was 'Herbie'. Only the name has been changed to protect the guilty. Herbie was a bit of an oddball, an elderly provincial reporter who turned up to every event looking exactly the same. He wore thick horn-rimmed glasses; a long dark overcoat, woollen scarf, deerstalker hat and Sherlock Holmes pipe. He was a relic of some bygone age, but no-one could remember which age.

His final assignment before he retired was a European cup-tie in Germany. The night before the match the press corps were to be found in their customary haunt, the hotel bar. Herbie, never a drinker and certainly not a womanizer, was spotted sitting at a table chatting away to a rather large German 'lady of leisure'. It can be safely assumed that the topic of conversation was either the weather, language differences, or possibly the match – certainly nothing at all improper.

No-one is now sure whose bright idea it was, but a decision was taken to send Herbie out in a blaze of glory. A whip-round was taken and Herbie was lured out of the room on the pretext that he was wanted on the phone. The lady was then quickly propositioned and despatched to Herbie's room. Returning to the bar to find his companion gone, Herbie finished his drink and, with a characteristic doff of his cap, went off to bed.

To this day, none of those present has the slightest idea what happened when Herbie got to his room to discover his unexpected going-away present. What people did notice, though, was that the following morning Herbie sat all through breakfast with an unaccustomed smile on his face.

SCOTLAND ON TOUR

eople have been unkind enough to suggest that Scots do not travel well. By 'Scots' they mean not just the admittedly boisterous Tartan Armies who decorate our sidelines, but the international squad also.

There has been the *occasional* incident, I will admit. The trouble is, people don't understand what the players have to put up with – the boredom and terrible food, the prison-like accommodation, all thousands of miles from home. At least, it was when Scotland went to Argentina in 1978.

Even today, there are two schools of thought about what was really going on when the pride of Scotland was arrested in the dead of night, halfway over a security fence. Were these brave lads really attempting to break out of their training camp, as one school suggested, or were they genuinely trying to get back in, as they themselves claimed, having been accidentally locked out after a harmless late-evening stroll? Anyone who had seen the barren state of their Colditz-style accommodation, the unfilled swimming pool, the unpainted walls and the sketchy plumbing, would not find it hard to believe that they were actually trying to escape. Either way, the newspapers had a field day.

There had been a little trouble four years earlier, on the way to the World Cup finals in West Germany. This also excited a lot of wild comment in the press. What really happened was very mild really, apart from the early-morning boat trip, the usual escape attempt, the hurricane inside the hotel . . .

Wee man in a boat

Scotland's World Cup began during the home international tournament. We trained together as a squad for about ten days and then, on a Tuesday evening, we met Wales at Hampden Park. Our big match was the one against England, the following Saturday. We were staying at Largs, and after the Welsh match our manager, Willie Ormond, allowed us all to relax in our own way.

Quite a large group of us decided to go over to a nearby hotel for a few drinks. We had intended to be back at our own hotel by midnight, but one thing led to another and it was beginning to get light when we were finally making our way home along the beach. Everyone was in good spirits, laughing and joking and generally larking about when we stumbled upon a small rowing boat. Before anyone really knew what had happened, Jimmy Johnstone had stepped into it and was bobbing about on the waves, just a few feet from the shore.

Jimmy sat down in the boat and started to sing, and the rest of us stood on the shore cheering him on. A few objects were thrown into the water in Jimmy's direction and he did his best to splash us back. The singing continued.

After a while one or two of the lads began to wander back to our hotel and eventually the group left at the water's edge began to think that it was time to follow them. Only then did it dawn on us that the little boat was gradually drifting away from the shore. Jimmy was still sitting in the bottom of it, quite unconcerned, singing his head off.

'Hey, come back in,' we cried, but there was no response from Jimmy, apart from the uninterrupted singing, and the boat kept

drifting further away.

Now it also dawned on us that there weren't any oars in the boat, not that Jimmy was in any fit state to use them even if there had been. As we stood helplessly calling to him to come back, the strong tide was carrying him further and further out into the Clyde; soon he was little more than a speck on the horizon.

The commotion had now begun to attract some outside attention; windows began to open along the sea front. It was about then that I realized that all the other lads except me had disappeared back into the hotel. As I stood there on the shore I was not entirely alone. Willie Ormond had been aroused by the din and was standing on the hotel steps on the opposite side of the road. As Jimmy vanished over the horizon to the strains of 'Scotland the Brave', I went over to Willie and said, rather lamely: 'I think we'd better call out the coastguard.'

A little while later, the stillness of the Largs early morning was broken by the gentle chug-chugging noise of the old coastguard vessel searching the Firth of Clyde for Jimmy. By some miracle they found him, still in the boat and still singing his heart out. An hour or so later they brought him back to the hotel. He was wearing only a vest and trousers and was blue with cold. If the Celtic supporters could have seen him at that moment they would have lynched him.

Naturally, later that morning there had to be an inquest. The Scottish footballing press – known to us as the 'Mafia' – had heard of the incident and wanted an explanation. A press conference was called.

After some food and drink and a few hours' sleep, Jimmy looked a good deal better, but he didn't fancy facing the music alone. The 'Mafia' are not noted for their sense of humour on these occasions and Jimmy wanted some moral support. He took me on one side.

'You'd better come in with me, big man,' he said. 'Give me a bit of help.'

'Not likely,' I said, 'it was you who went out in the boat. It wasn't my idea.'

'Come on, big man,' he pleaded, 'I'm a wee bit afraid of going in on my own.'

'All right,' I said, reluctantly, 'I'll come in with you, but don't get me involved.'

So we went into the hotel lounge together, where the grim-faced media men were waiting for us. It was a formidable scene; there were reporters, lights, television cameras, microphones and photographers; it was just like one of those American Senate investigations.

We sat down, Jimmy with his head bowed waiting for someone to set the ball rolling. Then came the first question: 'Tell us about the escapade, then. What happened?'

Without looking up, Jimmy replied, in a subdued voice: 'Denis and I decided to go fishing.'

I couldn't believe it. With his very first words he'd roped me in. And what was he talking about anyway. No oars, no fishing tackle, not even a sweater on his back – and he'd been fishing. That evening I telephoned my wife Di, and all I could hear on the line was her scornful voice repeating over and over: 'Fishing? Fishing?'

Despite what had happened, Willie Ormond resisted pressure to drop Jimmy from the team to play England; I was not in the side at the time, so the question of my playing did not arise. But Jimmy went out at Hampden Park and had an outstanding game. Scotland beat the Auld Enemy 2–0, and all was forgiven; beat England and anything can be forgiven!

The road to Germany

So we set off for Europe, where we were to play friendly matches against Belgium and Norway in the run-up to the World Cup finals.

A few days later we were staying in a very pleasant hotel in Antwerp. I had decided to get an early night, but I hadn't been in bed long when there was a knock at the bedroom door. It turned out to be Jimmy Johnstone and Billy Bremner who wanted to come in 'for a cup of tea and a chat'.

'Not likely,' I said, knowing that once they were inside they would have talked all night and I would never have got rid of them. I was determined to get some sleep.

The knocking continued. 'Come on, open up,' they kept calling out.

'Away to your beds', I replied, and pulled the sheets up around my ears. After a while, the knocking stopped and as silence descended on my room I drifted towards sleep.

I hadn't quite fallen asleep when I became aware that again people were outside my bedroom door. At first I could just make out the sound of whispering voices, then I began to hear a strange squeaking noise. I wondered what the hell was going on. The door was fitted with one of those peephole devices which allow you to look outside without opening the door, so I hopped out of bed to take a peep.

At first all I could see was the apparently deserted corridor, but then the strange squeaking noise started up again and I realized that it was coming from somewhere near the bottom of the door. Then I spotted Jimmy and Billy, crouched down on the carpet, barely visible through the spy hole.

'Hey, what are you two up to?' I called out, but there was no reply. The strange squeaking noise continued. Only when the door suddenly started to move did I realize that they had got hold of a screwdriver and were unscrewing the hinges from the outside. The bottom was now loose and they stood to get to work on the top hinge. As I watched through the peephole, I was glad to see another figure appear in the background. It was the hotel manager.

Poor Willie Ormond had to be sent for and once again Jimmy was in trouble. Fortunately, on this occasion the press were not aware of the incident which passed off quietly after the boys had collected a ticking off from Willie. Jimmy, though, was still smarting over the treatment the newspapers had given him after the boat escapade, and this was to lead to trouble a few nights later, when we were in Oslo.

Jimmy and Billy were sitting in the hotel bar, already having had one or two, when some of the pressmen walked in. Very soon after that a row developed as Jimmy sounded off at the press lads and Billy pitched in with a few supporting verbals. At one point the row looked as if it might go beyond words, so some of the other players stepped in and eventually persuaded the two terriers to leave it alone and go to bed. They left rather reluctantly, complaining that they were 'fed up'.

That, we thought, was the end of it; but not so. A short while later, as I was going to my room, I met the pair of them staggering along a corridor dragging a couple of enormous suitcases behind them.

'Where the hell are you two going?' I asked.

'Home,' was the flat reply.

'Home where?' I asked.

'Home to Scotland,' they said, 'we've had enough'.

I was speechless: here they were, planning to decamp in the middle of the night.

A quick solution was called for and a nearby service room provided it. I managed to bundle them inside and lock the door. They needed time to cool off.

Meanwhile, the pressmen had complained to Willie Ormond about the row in the bar and once again there was a hue and cry on for the terrible twins. Through the service-room door a hasty pact was agreed, and the following morning there was another meeting with the press but this time common sense prevailed. Everyone concerned agreed to play the incident down and put the past behind them. After all, in just a few more days we were due to play our first World Cup match. Sanity broke through at last.

The World Cup itself passed off without incident, and although we were eliminated at the end of the first stage we had performed well. A victory over Zaire, followed by drawn matches against Brazil and Yugoslavia, meant that we went out of the competition on goal difference. Scotland were in fact the only team in the 1974 World Cup not to lose a match. Even the eventual winners, West Germany, lost 1–0 to East Germany in the first stage. We were to go home disappointed, but at least with our heads held high.

That ought to have been the end of the excitement, but it wasn't. With just one day left before we returned home, I was sitting at the bar of our Frankfurt hotel enjoying a quiet drink. I had done all my shopping and almost completed my packing, so I was feeling fairly content. I was looking forward to a good night's rest, then we would be off home the following day.

I was somewhere in a daydream when I became aware of furtive movements behind me. I spun round to see seven or eight of the lads about to spring. The next instant they had grabbed me and I was carried off through the hotel. I suddenly had a nasty feeling about where they were taking me.

A feature of the hotel was the beautiful swimming pool right in the centre. Most of the lads had spent a good deal of time there but, being a non-swimmer, I had not been near it. Now we were heading in that direction. I was grabbing hold of everything in sight, trying desperately to find something to cling onto, but to no avail. There were far too many of them, and they were much too powerful for me. I pleaded with them to put me down but they wouldn't listen.

They got me to the side of the pool – fully clothed – and then I was held by the arms and legs and swung out over the water. One, two, three . . . I was absolutely terrified, but I still couldn't believe that they would actually throw me in. After all, they knew that I couldn't swim.

The next instant I was flying through the air and my whole life went past in a flash. A second later I was in the water. I was aware that two of them had come in with me to make sure that I was all right, and then I realized that the water was less than five feet deep. I could stand up in it in perfect safety.

Dripping wet and feeling a little shell-shocked, I scrambled out and squelched off back to my room in search of dry clothing, only to find another surprise in store. The lads had been there before me.

The room looked as if it had been hit by a hurricane. The furniture was upside down and all of my neatly packed bags had been opened and the contents scattered everywhere. It was a shambles. So much for my preparations for going home.

The horseplay went on for most of that night as the lads let off steam. One by one they all ended up in the pool, literally soaking the tensions of an arduous tour out of their systems. It was an appropriate ending, too, for Scotland's Watery World Cup, begun that morning not so long ago beside the Firth of Clyde.

AMERICAN DREAMS

he ball was played through the midfield. I latched on to it and headed towards the penalty area. Suddenly there was an excruciating pain in my left ankle and I fell to the ground in a heap. An opposing defender had kicked my feet from under me. As I lay on the ground, watching the 'assassin' make off with the ball, it slowly began to dawn on me that this was the sort of thing I could expect if I was going to make guest appearances in pro-celebrity teams. There would always be some cowboy on the other side out to make a name for himself. I decided there and then that this was not for me.

That was in 1974, soon after I had retired. It was one of the first of many such invitations I had accepted. Now, I had to think of some way to get out of the rest. I had never enjoyed getting kicked while I was being well paid for it, and I was damned if I was going to put up with it for 'fun'. I decided to limit my future 'appearances' to the few that had any real meaning, such as benefit matches for former colleagues.

That year was a time of decision for me. After I had given up playing, I declined several offers to go into football management because I feel that the manager's job is the worst one in football. It may be fine when things are going well, but it is hell when they're not, and there is only a thin line between the two.

One of the more attractive offers I received was to play football in the United States, but it was a couple of seasons before the Americans began offering really big money. Bearing in mind that it was a short season and I would have to have some other job for the rest of the year, what was on offer at the time was not quite enough to tempt me. When I saw what was paid, a year or two later, to Pele and George Best, Beckenbauer, Cruyff, and to some far less talented players, I couldn't help feeling that I'd hung up my boots too soon.

By the end of the Seventies, the American scene was in full swing, and the stories that came back across the Atlantic made me curious to see for myself what it was like. When a group of friends asked me to go on a trip to California, in the summer of 1981, I was very keen to go. The party was made up of some former players, old friends like Ian St John and Roger Hunt, and one or two of my new friends from the world of radio and television: Alan Parry, John Motson, Jim Rosenthal, Martin Tyler, David Hamilton and one or two others. The one snag was that they wanted me to play a couple of matches in their pro-celebrity team.

My mind went back to that day in 1974. I could almost feel the pain in my ankle. I certainly wanted to go on the trip, but I was equally determined that I didn't want to play. Apart from anything else I wasn't fit; I hadn't trained for over six years. In the end a compromise was reached. It was agreed that I should go as the team's honorary manager.

I'd heard a lot about this great team they had. I'd heard all about the 'great runs', the 'delicately chipped balls' and the 'beautiful headers'. I was quite looking forward to seeing them for myself. What a surprise I had in store.

The former pros were all right, of course, but the rest of them were a revelation. Rosey played the first match of the tour as if he had two left feet, Martin Tyler didn't seem to be able to see the ball properly, Parry made the infamous Rattin look like an angel, and as for poor old Motty, well!

It will never cease to amaze me how a group of blokes who care so much about the game, who eat, sleep and drink it and never stop analyzing it, could be so clueless on the field. (No doubt they have their own views of me as a commentator!) As their manager, of course, I was expected to sit and watch them. I thought: 'What have I done to deserve this?'

The one consolation was that the weather was glorious, and I noticed that the far side of the pitch was bathed in sunshine. Over there, too, was a nice handy bench which no-one was using. I decided to make the most of it. I took off my shirt and stretched out to soak up the sun. From time to time I called words of encouragement to my team: 'Come on lads, get stuck in.'

The sun on my skin felt terrific. After a while I closed my eyes and let myself really relax. The next thing I knew, someone was waking me up to tell me that the match was over. It must be the first time in the history of football that a manager has fallen asleep during a match.

The highlight of our trip was a visit to a North American League match. We went, as guests of the club, to watch Tampa Bay Rowdies play Montreal. It was an experience I'll never forget.

We arrived an hour and a half before the game to find thousands of people having barbecue lunches in the huge grassed car parks. There was acres of room for everyone to park and whole families were setting up their own individual barbecues at the side of

their cars.

The stadium was beautiful, everything clean and freshly painted. Inside there was a carnival atmosphere, as though everyone was on holiday. We had the choice of either sitting in one of the club's private boxes or finding a place in the crowd. I decided to sit in the crowd. On the pitch a large brass band was playing while the girl majorettes went through their dance routines. A Mickey Mouse character was running up and down the stadium steps entertaining the kids. All the while, white-suited vendors were doing the rounds selling drinks, hamburgers, hot dogs, popcorn, sweets and anything else you could think of. It was a uniquely American occasion. The whole purpose seemed to be pure enjoyment; of tensions or crowd anger there was not a sign.

Shortly before the kick-off, the two teams were introduced. Each player was called onto the field by a public address announcement and given an individual round of applause.

Once the game was under way, one of the most striking things to a newcomer was that the movement on the terraces never ceased. The vendors were still selling their popcorn; Mickey Mouse was still running up and down the stairs; people were moving about; and down at the side of the pitch the forty-strong band was still beating out its rhythm. There was a commentary as well, but the commentator only seemed to know the names of three or four players, so at times it sounded as though some players were passing to themselves.

They also had an organ, which piped out a repetitive tune rather like the ones that accompanied the old silent comedy films. Whenever Tampa attacked, the tempo of the organ music increased, building to a crescendo if a goal was scored, or dramatically fading away when a chance was missed.

There seemed to be no end to the inventiveness of the organizers. Throughout the afternoon new attractions were brought in, as when, during the second half, eight of the bandsmen broke away from the main group and began playing dixie behind one of the goals. All the while the match went on in the centre of the stadium.

The football itself was of fairly poor quality. They played with offside lines 35 yards from each end of the pitch, which meant that most of the play took place in the middle third of the field. Every so often one or other of the teams would make a breakaway and there would be a rush towards one of the goals. It seemed to me that they had most things right off the field, but not on it; the presentation and packaging were great, but the product didn't look so good when the wrappers were off.

Soccer in the United States must have come as a boon to smaller men. After all, you need to be at least six feet tall to play basketball, and weigh not less than eighteen stone to play grid-iron football. Our brand of the game gave a chance to the little men. Perhaps for that reason alone it might survive in the States. Certainly, though, it's a lot different from the game we were brought up on. Just how different, Trevor Hockey could probably explain as well as anyone.

When he left Sheffield United to join an American club, he was given an unusual welcome by his new fans. They drove him into the stadium dressed as a general, sitting in the back of a jeep. Imagine a scene like that at Bramall Lane.

THE COMMENTATORS

he radio commentator was getting excited. It was an FA Cup-tie, at Selhurst Park, and an upset was on the cards. First Division Crystal Palace were at home to Second Division Swansea and the Welshmen were leading 2–1. Suddenly the ball was in the net again and the commentator went into overdrive.

'It's there, a great goal,' he roared. 'Swansea lead 3–1 – what a night for the Second Division club . . . they'll be singing in the valleys tonight. It's Swansea 3, Crystal Palace . . .' The voice trailed away to nothing, then picked up again, hesitantly now. 'No, it's Palace who've scored, so that makes it 2–2.'

Every commentator's worst nightmare had become reality. A momentary loss of concentration, wires in the brain were crossed, and the wrong words came out of his mouth. If you're in the business, you don't laugh. Tomorrow it could happen to you.

The radio commentary team I worked with, at the BBC, used a system whereby the producer passed important notes to his commentator written on the back of a postcard. The commentator would then find a brief pause in his commentary, glance down to read the card and digest whatever instruction he had been given, and carry on. Generally the system worked very well. But it could go wrong.

A couple of seasons ago, England were playing Spain in Barcelona. Commentary was scheduled for the second half only, and all through the first half a Spanish fan was beating a huge drum just a few feet from the commentary position. The drumming was so loud that the producer felt his commentator would have to explain the noise when they eventually went on the air.

Half-time arrived and the commentary team went on the air, but by now the drumming had stopped, so there was no longer any need to mention it. Several minutes into the second half, however, it started up again and the producer decided it would have to be explained. The only man who seemed unaware of the thud–thud–thudding was the commentator, now wholly engrossed in the match. So the producer wrote on one of his cards: 'Mention the drummer,' and placed the card in front of the commentator. A few seconds later he glanced down at the card, then came out with this remarkable piece of commentary:

'And the ball is inside the penalty area, mention the drummer,

a great shot there, by
Stevie Coppell, coming in on the far side.'

Mention of the card system reminds me of one of my own
worst moments. We were at Highbury, where Arsenal were playing
Brighton. It was Brighton's first season in the First Division and they
were getting slaughtered 4–0. There wasn't really very much that
could be said about their performance which was favourable.

The radio commentary position at Highbury is in the front
row of the directors' box and we were surrounded by Brighton
directors and officials. As the game went on I was becoming more
and more conscious that the only things we were saying about
Brighton were uncomplimentary. The one positive thing I could think
of to say was that their central defender, Mark Lawrenson, whom I
hadn't seen before, was having a fine game.

I picked up my microphone and said: 'Well, at least Brighton
have the consolation that they do have a very bright prospect in this
young central defender, Mark Lawrenson. I'm sure that if he carries

on playing as well as he has today, it won't be long before Ron Greenwood gives him a chance in the England team.'

I put the microphone down and sat back feeling pretty pleased with myself.

A moment later, our producer slipped a card in front of me. On it he had written: 'Mark Lawrenson has already played 5 times for the Republic of Ireland.' Have you ever wished that the ground would open up and swallow you?

All broadcasting is a matter of teamwork. No one person carries the show on his or her own, and commentators in particular are continually in need of support and the goodwill of others. One of the most bizarre situations I can remember illustrates the point well.

We were in Paris for the 1981 European Cup Final. Liverpool were due to meet Real Madrid. Everything had gone well on the trip until we learned, on the afternoon of the match, that a French works department bulldozer had sliced through a large number of post office cables and all our broadcasting circuits to London had been lost. The French post office were doing everything they could to repair the damage, but they were not optimistic about restoring our circuits in time for the kick-off, at 7.30 pm.

Our producer went on the telephone to London and it was agreed that, if all else failed, we would attempt to do the commentary on the telephone. The problem here was, the purpose-built commentary box had no telephone. An English journalist had offered to lend us his telephone in the press box, which he wouldn't be using while the match was in progress. But the press box was fifty or sixty yards from the commentary position, so this was not a lot of use. Our main hope was that proper broadcasting-quality circuits would be restored in time.

BBC Radio Merseyside had also booked circuits to do their own commentary, but they were in the same boat as the Radio 2 team. It was agreed, therefore, that if just one set of circuits could be restored, the Radio 2 boys would use them, and Radio Merseyside would simply take the Radio 2 commentary.

For more than an hour before the match we took it in turns to call London from each of the two positions, while our producer, Ron Gubba, was up and down the stairs like a yoyo making telephone calls from the press box to find out if the radio engineers at Broadcasting House were picking up either of the signals.

Normally a broadcasting circuit consists of two wires, one to carry the commentary out of the stadium, the other to provide what we call 'cue programme' to the commentator's headphones so that he can hear the announcer in London and know when he is due to speak. The French post office had warned us that if we were lucky enough to get anything at all, it was likely to be only a single wire to carry the commentary. This meant that the commentator would have to broadcast 'blind', as it were. A way round this under normal circumstances would be to take 'cue' from the telephone, but our nearest telephone was fifty or sixty yards away in the press box.

Miraculously, less than five minutes before the kick-off, word came through that the engineers in London were hearing one of our commentators, but they hadn't been able to identify the voice and therefore weren't sure which of the two positions might be working. In the few moments that remained it was decided that our two commentators, Alan Parry and Peter Jones, would start up simultaneously on the stroke of 7.30, one in each of the two positions. The producer had telephone contact with London from the press box, which fortunately was visible from the commentary position. He would indicate by a hand signal which, if either, of our two commentators was on the air. If he raised his right hand, that would mean that the engineers in London were hearing Alan Parry, the left hand would mean they were hearing Peter Jones. A wave of both hands meant they were hearing neither.

The moment arrived and both men started their commentary as if everything was perfectly normal. A second or two later, up went the producer's right arm to indicate that Alan Parry was on the air. No-one in the listening audience could have had the slightest inkling of the drama which had gone on beforehand. Needless to say, we were all elated; magic moments such as those are what make broadcasting so exciting.

Problems arise at home as well as abroad, of course, but somehow they seem more bizarre when they happen abroad. Language difficulties often have something to do with this, as they did when we were in France for a match between St Etienne and Manchester United.

Normally, for a radio broadcast, we would have four microphones, four headsets, various small amplifiers and a couple of engineers to 'balance' the sound. The BBC has reciprocal arrangements with foreign broadcasting organizations whereby the home country provides engineering services for its visitors. We service their broadcasts in Britain, and vice versa.

For the St Etienne match we arrived at our commentary position to find a couple of bared wires marked BBC, but no sign of any other equipment. Then a French radio engineer arrived and said to our producer: 'Où ést votre equipement?'

Not speaking French, the producer looked puzzled, but Peter Jones had grasped the gist of it and said to the producer: 'I think he's asking you where your equipment is.'

'Oh gawd,' said the producer.

What had happened was, the last BBC producer to visit St Etienne had brought BBC microphones with him, because he preferred them to the ones provided by the French. The French engineer had taken that to mean that in future the BBC would bring their own equipment with them. When he realized that we hadn't brought any, there was a frantic chase back to his base to pick up the necessary bits and pieces, which only arrived in the nick of time.

Who needs seats?

Someone new to the commentating trade might think that the bigger the match, the better the facilities. More often than not, the reverse is true. There were so many visiting broadcasters at the 1978 World

Cup, for instance, that the Argentines wanted to limit each broadcasting organization to two seats. Since the BBC Radio commentary team was a four-man outfit, this posed a few problems.

For some of the less important matches, we were able to wangle two extra positions, which solved the problem, but when Argentina were scheduled to meet Italy at the River Plate Stadium, in the final match of the first group stage, there was no question of spare seats. This was a match which everyone wanted to be at and so, although we could get our four-man team into the stadium, we were allocated just one commentary position.

This actually consisted of three seats, but the middle one of the three was piled high with broadcasting equipment and was impossible to sit on. To each side of our position was a row of concrete steps. We decided that the producer would sit on the steps on one side of the position and I would sit next to him in one of the seats. The two commentators would alternate between sitting in the other seat and on the steps, according to who was commentating at the time. The system was that one commentator would cover the first quarter of the match and then hand over to the other, who would take the commentary up to half-time. They would do the same in the second half. My contribution as the 'expert' was to give summaries when needed and comment on any interesting moments as they arose.

Midway through the first half, the ball went out of play and the two commentators began the awkward process of changing places, which involved the outgoing man handing his headset to the incoming one. While this was going on I was holding the fort, talking about the pattern of the match so far. So far so good, but then to my horror Italy took a very quick throw-in, Rossi backheeled the ball to Bettega and a second later it was in the back of Argentina's net. My two colleagues were still in the process of changing places, and in the confusion no-one described, or even mentioned, what proved to be the only goal of the match. Naturally, people back home were unaware of our difficulties and the following day there were angry messages from London demanding to know what had gone wrong. After that fiasco we had a change of policy. The two commentators sat in the comfortable seats and I sat, like the producer, on a cold step.

While we were operating from Buenos Aires, we had a primitive but adequate prefabricated studio inside the unfinished shell of the city's new broadcasting complex. At our other centres, though, such as Cordoba where the Scotland team did their training, we had to make the best use we could of the hotel bedroom.

In Cordoba, we decided to use the tiny bathroom of one of the

hotel rooms as our studio. 'Try to forget the surroundings,' Peter Jones advised me. 'Just remember our broadcasts will be going out to people while they are driving home from work, so try to make it sound as natural as possible.'

That was a bit difficult since Bryon Butler was sitting on the edge of the bath, holding the telephone, and I was sitting on the toilet. Our very first broadcast in fact lived up to the ramshackle surroundings in which it was made. Jim Rosenthal was linking the programme from our studio in Buenos Aires. He did the opening headlines and then it was our turn. I could hear Jim cueing us in: 'And now, with news of Scotland's preparations our reporters in Cordoba, Denis Law and Bryon Butler.'

At that moment I leaned back heavily and flushed the toilet with my left elbow. I don't know if anyone heard it back home, but where I was it sounded like a thunderstorm.

The next night, we decided to switch things around. Bryon would sit on the toilet and I would sit on the edge of the bath. Because a bathroom can sound like an echo chamber, we had drawn the shower curtains across in an effort to dampen the sound. This time, just as Jim cued over to us, I fell over backwards into the bath. The curtain rings snapped off one by one in quick succession, making a noise like muffled rifle shots. (And now, from our man in front of the firing squad: 'Aaaaaaghh!')

Of all the people I've worked with, no-one has a livelier mind nor a sharper wit than Alan Parry. I remember one night when our four-man commentary team was at Burnden Park, where Bolton were playing Nottingham Forest in a League Cup match. It was a bitterly cold night and I had turned up in a flimsy windcheater, which was nowhere near warm enough. I'm used to people making comments about my nose, but on this occasion it was blue. I was frozen through.

Alan and the rest of us had already had a bit of a laugh about my plight before we went on the air, but then in the middle of the broadcast, during a lull in play, he announced to the listening world: 'This seems to be a good moment to launch the "buy a coat for Denis Law" appeal.' He went on to explain the remark, with the rest of us splitting our sides in the background.

At Anfield one day we were scheduled to do a second-half commentary on a League match between Liverpool and Manchester United. Before we actually went into the commentary sequence, Alan had to do a forty-five second report on the first half, which had been a thriller. At the time, Abba were top of the hit parade, and as

ho's turned e ☆⊙M⊛✕ up on ?!

he went on the air one of their records was being played, rather loudly, over the public-address system. Aware that the listeners at home could obviously hear the music, Alan ended his report with the words: 'Forty-five minutes of the best football I've seen this season, and now Abba. This must be what paradise is like.' The rest of us collapsed in a heap.

Trials of a TV commentator

The television commentator doesn't need to talk as much as his radio counterpart, because very often the pictures will tell the story better on their own; but he does need at least three eyeballs. Two are for watching a television monitor beside him and the other one is for following the live action. If he can't do this, he may find himself talking about something that isn't being shown. John Motson is one who can do it, and very well, but even he gets in an occasional tangle, as when last season he was commentating on a match involving Manchester United and came out with the words: 'Just look at Robson, making a brilliant run – out of your picture.'

A much more tricky problem occurred a couple of seasons ago at Maine Road, Manchester, where City were playing Liverpool in the semi-final of the League Cup. Normally, slow-motion replays are edited into a recording after the match is over, but with evening matches there is not enough time before transmission and they have to be played into the main recording as they happen.

On the night in question, Manchester City scored a 'goal' very early in the match, only to have it surprisingly disallowed for some fairly harmless pushing which had taken place as the ball was in flight. Not wanting to give the referec time to change his decision, Liverpool took the free-kick very quickly, and the match was restarted in a matter of seconds.

Meanwhile, on the television gantry, the commentator was watching the slow-motion replay of the 'goal' and adding some further words over the replay. By the time he looked back to the pitch the game had been restarted, and neither he nor anyone in the TV team realized that the goal had been disallowed.

The first inkling they had of this came at half-time when the runner, who relays information up from the dressing-room area, said on his walkie-talkie that he now had information from the referee about why the 'goal' had been disallowed. Pandemonium on the gantry! After the match a certain well-known commentator had to re-record whole sections of his first-half commentary, removing all references to 'City's one-nil lead'. Fortunately for everyone concerned, that was the only 'goal' scored in the first half, otherwise the task might have been impossible in the time that was available.

As a player-turned-interviewer, I can now well understand some of the difficulties facing the lads who stand on the touchline with a microphone at the end of a match. Many of today's players are articulate and well educated, but there are also still plenty who find difficulty in stringing three words together. My heart sinks when it's my turn and the biggest 'Yes/No' merchant on the park slips in his fourth goal of the night. I know that he's got to be interviewed and I'm on a hiding to nothing.

Many of the more successful managers and players have, through practice, become experienced interviewees and will avoid such phrases as 'over the moon' or 'sick as a parrot', which are now as much of a joke inside the dressing-room as outside it. But there are still a great many who will tell you that 'it was a game of two halves,' or that 'the lads battled really well', or that they 'didn't get the run of the ball' or that 'after they scored, we had a mountain to climb', or that . . . zzzzz.

Television studios can be very daunting places if you are not used to them. To the untutored eye it seems that everywhere there is chaos, with droves of people all busily doing different things and all talking at once. There are camera men, sound men, lighting men, wardrobe assistants, scene hands, floor managers, directors, producers and a host of others, all with important roles in the whole operation.

Once the show gets started, the studio becomes quiet – but now the chaos is going on in the ear of the person in front of the camera. Voices calling 'Run VT,' girls counting 'Ten, nine, eight, seven, six, five . . . ,' the director saying 'Cue so and so.' That it usually all comes out looking so polished and relaxed, reflects great credit on the dozens of unseen people behind the cameras.

In a sports programme, the main role of the person in front of the camera – the link man – is to lead in to the various programme items which may be on film but are more usually on videotape, or VT as it is called. When the director or his assistant says 'Run VT,' that usually means that in ten seconds time the appropriate pictures will appear on the screen. The link man knows that he has ten seconds in which to lead to the pictures with appropriate words. All the while, in his ear, a girl is counting the pictures in: 'Ten, nine, eight, seven, six . . .'

The script for these critically timed links is usually prepared in advance in order to work out the timing. That's fine when things go according to plan, but unfortunately the plans sometimes go astray. Machinery can let you down.

Once, when I was very new to all this, I was leading to a piece of VT when the machinery did fail. I came to the end of my link with the words: 'Fulham are in the dark shorts.' I turned to look at the monitor, but to my horror nothing had happened. Now I could hear the director's voice in my ear saying 'Keep going, the VT has failed.'

I was panic-stricken. It had never occurred to me that I might need to say more than I already had. Now I was completely dry. I just froze. Keep going with what? I thought.

Fortunately I had an experienced colleague in the studio who saw my dilemma and took over the responsibility for keeping the show on the road. I've seldom felt more grateful to anyone than I did to him in that moment. Afterwards, of course, when I sat down and thought about it calmly, I could think of a dozen things I might have said, and the next time I met that particular crisis, I knew what to do.

The people in the studio told me that such things only happened once in a blue moon. All I can say is that blue moons seem to occur on average once a fortnight!

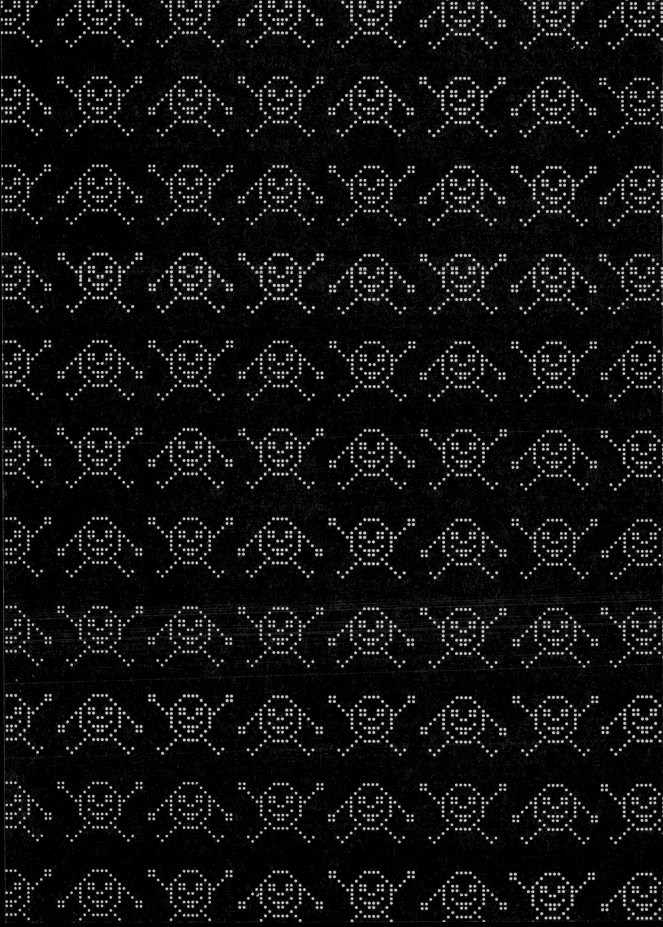